Lessons for Becoming a Great Conversationalist

Master Debate

Myeong-Hee Seong
Casey Freeman

지식인

Profile

Myeong-Hee Seong

Ph.D. in English Education, Korea University

Casey Freeman

M.A. in Journalism, University of Colorado
Professor, Eulji University

Master Debate

Lessons for Becoming a Great Conversationalist

2013년 8월 15일 초판 1쇄 발행
2020년 8월 25일 초판 6쇄 발행

지은이 | Myeong-Hee Seong · Casey Freeman
펴낸이 | 김종욱 · 명사동
펴낸곳 | 지식인
등 록 | 제301-2013-134호
주 소 | 서울시 도봉구 도봉로 180길 20 투웨니퍼스트 102동 602호
전 화 | 02)2266-8606
팩 스 | 02)2266-8607
E-mail | jisikin2013@naver.com
홈페이지 | www.jisikinbook.co.kr

ISBN 978-89-98591-07-6 (93740)

값 13,000원

Master Debate

Lessons for Becoming a Great Conversationalist

CONTENTS

Master

Lessons for Becoming a Great Conversationalist

Debate

Unit 1

The Right Age for Alcohol

UNIT 1

ICEBREAKERS

- If you drink, how old were you when you and your friends started drinking alcohol?
- What do you think the legal drinking age should be? Why?
- Should people take a test to see if they are mature enough to drink alcohol? Why or why not?

RAPID FIRE

Brainstorm words or sentences related to drinking.

	Words	Sentences
Noun	Ex) Alcohol, liquor,	
Verb	Ex) To drink,	
Adjective	Ex) Intoxicated,	

VOCABULARY PREVIEW

Fill in the blank with proper words using the following words.

Mingle	Accents	Monitor	Establishment
Pronunciation	Legislation	Stupor	Creep out

1. People from different areas of the country speak with different __________.
2. The principal needed to __________ the students during recess.
3. The gas leak caused a __________ for the factory workers.
4. The waiters at that __________ were rude to my mother, so I will not go back.
5. I think it is important for everybody to __________ during parties.

IDIOM TIME! *Connect the idioms with their meanings.*

Learning idioms will help you sound more like a native speaker, but also, they're fun! Check out these idioms. What do they mean? When would you use them?

Idiom	Meaning
1. Beer goggles	a. rank very high
2. Wrap around a telephone pole	b. making bad decisions while drunk
3. Top the charts	c. stupid
4. Thick skulled	d. crash a car
5. Use as a crutch	e. to need something to accomplish a task

Write three sentences with any of the idioms we learned about today.

1. ____

2. ____

3. ____

CONVERSATION

TALKING TIPS

These skills will make you a better English speaker and listener. Pay attention!

Don't Worry, Just Do It

One thing that stops Koreans from learning English is the fear of not speaking perfect English. Most native English speakers understand that English is an incredibly difficult language to learn, and don't expect anybody to use perfect grammar. So instead of worrying about sounding fluent, go ahead and just talk to people. This will help your confidence and you will become a better English user. The only way to learn to speak English better is to actually speak English.

TALKING TIME

Practice this couple's conversation about alcohol using Talking Tips.

BETSY Roberto, why don't you go mingle with the other people at this party?

ROBERTO Oh, I don't know. My English is not great.

BETSY Who cares? You can always just talk to somebody.

ROBERTO But what if I make a mistake?

BETSY Seriously, it doesn't matter. I make mistakes every day. The New York Times makes grammar mistakes.

ROBERTO I am also worried about my accent.

BETSY Everybody who speaks English has some kind of accent. Whether you're from England, Ireland, Wales, Scotland, Australia, New Zealand, the USA or Canada. There are a million accents.

ROBERTO And my pronunciation?

BETSY Again, people in America who live across the street from each other speak differently.

ROBERTO Maybe if I drink a little bit more I will feel good enough to talk to them.

BETSY That's using alcohol like a crutch. If you only talk when you're drunk, you'll never talk to anybody when you're sober.

ROBERTO I get so nervous though.

BETSY When you do anything the first time, you will probably be nervous. Just go and do it!

QUESTION TIME

Now answer these questions about the dialog.

1. Why is Roberto so nervous?

2. What advice does Betsy give to Roberto?

3. What does Roberto think will make him less nervous?

4. Why does Betsy want Roberto to stay sober?

5. What are other things that you think Roberto can do to make him less nervous?

TOPIC STORY

Read this story and talk about the most interesting things in the story.

The Right Age for Alcohol

Student and parent groups at the University of Colorado-Boulder (CU) are asking lawmakers to consider the State of Colorado's past legislation with alcohol. Some people are asking the state to lower the drinking age, but only to allow younger people to drink beer or wine of lower-alcohol content.

"Instead of our children and students illegally purchasing alcohol that is too strong for them, why don't we allow them some experience with alcohol?" said Victoria Henze from Reforming Alcohol Laws. "Maybe this isn't the strongest booze they can get, but at least we can legalize it and we can monitor these young drinkers in proper bars."

About 30 years ago, students the age of 18 at CU could go to bars and drink "Kid Beer" or "3.2 Brew." This type of beer featured an alcohol content of only 3.2 percent. Regular beer averages an alcohol content of about 5 percent. Back then, 18-year-old drinkers could only buy this beer at certain bars, where security people monitored drinking activities.

The theory is that if students can drink in a controlled environment they would not overdrink, drive under the influence of alcohol, fight, lose consciousness or any other troubling activities related to alcohol.

"These young adults will drink anyway," said Henze. "We might as well let them. However, instead of them buying hard alcohol such as vodka or whiskey, we can allow them these ultra-light beers so they won't be drinking themselves into stupors or fighting or doing anything else stupid."

Opponents of this measure claim this is just a publicity stunt to sell more alcohol. "Why should we lower our drinking age? We already have people who drink under the age and wrap their cars around telephone poles," said Tyler Skitt from the Boulder Youth Department. "Now these idiots want to encourage the young people to drink. Why don't we just tell them not to drink at all?"

Back during the 1970s when 18 year olds could drink "Kid Beer," there were less alcohol violations and fatalities. In 2012, Colorado topped the charts with alcohol violations. Changing the law may allow other states to consider if this could be the right approach to alcohol. The United States sets the drinking age at 21 years old, one of the oldest in the world. South Koreans may drink at the age of 19, but most countries let people drink by the age of 18.

"We let people under 21 to fight and die in the military, but we won't let them have a beer? It's ridiculous," said Henze.

(Colorado Daily - Newspaper: November 11, 2012)

COMPREHENSION QUESTIONS

Answer the following questions and write complete sentences.

1. What rule is being considered for a change?

____

2. Why does Victoria Henze want to change this rule?

____

3. What does the opponent of this new rule think about it?

____

4. Which charts did Colorado top?

____

5. What is "Kid Beer?"

____

In a group, write and discuss what you think about drinking ages.

What do you think about drinking ages? Should the USA lower the drinking age? Does South Korea have a good drinking age? Did you ever drink before you were legally allowed to buy or drink alcohol? How did you obtain alcohol before you were old enough to drink?

____

____

____

____

____

HERE'S SOME MORE...

Read about culture from across the globe about today's topic.

Sorry, You're Too Old

While there is an age minimum to enter most clubs or bars in Korea, there is starting to be an age maximum! Some drinking establishments are checking the IDs of patrons not to see if they are too young, but to see if they are too old.

"This is totally insulting," said Boram Kim, a 33-year-old woman from Apgujeong who was refused entry into the Foundry, a dance club in Gangnam. "All I want to do is go into this place and dance and drink a few drinks with my friends. Now they are telling me I can't even do that? These owners are thick-skulled morons."

The places that enacted this rule say this is well within their rights to judge who may or may not enter their businesses.

"I want my dance floor to look good. If somebody doesn't look good or is too old, I don't want them there," said Matt Donahue, owner of the Foundry. "Also, older men tend to creep out some of the younger girls. So we don't want them there either. There are plenty of other bars these old weirdos can go and be weird."

Other hot spots separate the ages. There is an under-30 section and an over-30 section.

(Gangnam Gazette- Newspaper: April 19, 2013)

DYNAMITE DISCUSSION

Gather a group and discuss these following questions. When your group finishes, present your ideas to other students.

1. What do you think about separating people at bars due to ages?

2. What do you think about lowering the drinking age?

3. What types of alcohol do you like?

4. If you drink, where do you like to go: your home, the park, bars, clubs, parties or anywhere else?

5. What do you do if you see somebody who has drunk too much alcohol?

6. When do you like to drink? The weekend? Holidays? Every day or night?

7. Think about Korea's reputation with alcohol. How would you change it?

8. What are other things young people can do for fun besides drink?

9. What are some weird rules bars, clubs and pubs have?

10. Would you attend a club with separate sections for different ages of people? Why?

GET IT TOGETHER

Divide into two groups: one group the Pro team and the other the Con team. Write about the pros and cons of changing the drinking age. Then debate.

1. Would you buy alcohol for somebody that is too young to buy their own? Why or why not?

____

____

2. How should the government punish the people who supply alcohol to underage drinkers?

____

____

3. What are some pros of younger drinking ages? What are some cons?

Pros:

Cons:

M a s t e r

Lessons for Becoming a Great Conversationalist

D e b a t e

Master

Lessons for Becoming a Great Conversationalist

Debate

Unit

2

Disrupting Rest in Peace

UNIT 2

ICEBREAKERS

- Where would you like to be buried?
- How would you like to be buried? Why?
- Talk about funerals you have attended.

RAPID FIRE

Brainstorm words or sentences related to funerals.

	Words	Sentences
Noun	Ex) Burial, funeral,	
Verb	Ex) To die,	
Adjective	Ex) Deceased,	

VOCABULARY PREVIEW

Fill in the blank with proper words using the following words.

Console	Phrase	Casket	Acquaintance
Suffer	Revenues	Cremated	Grieving

1. Long before he became my __________, Alex and I didn't like each other much.
2. The family with their grandmother in the hospital will be __________ after she dies.
3. The company's __________ are down this year so I don't think we will receive bonuses.
4. Funeral planning is difficult because people do not expect to decide between the body being __________ or buried.
5. The coach will __________ the sad team after their big loss.

IDIOM TIME! *Connect the idioms with their meanings.*

Learning idioms will help you sound more like a native speaker, but also, they're fun! Check out these idioms. What do they mean? When would you use them?

1. A friend lost somebody	a. a phrase used to console
2. My heart goes out to you	b. things a person wants to do before they die
3. Rest in peace	c. to die
4. Kick the bucket	d. a person close to an acquaintance has died
5. Bucket list	e. a way to describe somebody who has died

Write three sentences with any of the idioms we learned about today.

1. ______________________________
2. ______________________________
3. ______________________________

CONVERSATION

TALKING TIPS

These skills will make you a better English speaker and listener. Pay attention!

Lessening The Pain

When somebody close to you loses a relative or friend, consoling them can be very difficult. Sometimes, we do not know what to say to make somebody feel better. Often, there is nothing to say to relieve some of the grief these people are feeling.

Here are a few phrases that you can use if someone you know suffers a death of a close acquaintance: *I am sorry for your loss*. This is probably the most common phrase we use in English. You can use this with just about any type of death. *My condolences*. This is just a very fancy way of saying, "I'm sorry." *My heart goes out to you*. This is another common but clever thing to say to somebody grieving. *If you need anything, or just need to talk, just ask*. Using this phrase may open you up to more responsibility, but this can be comforting for the suffering person to hear.

TALKING TIME

Practice this couple's conversation about funerals using Talking Tips.

LAURA	Ah, my dog bit the dust yesterday.
MIKE	Oh, I'm sorry for your loss.
LAURA	It's okay, he was getting old.
MIKE	What was his name?
LAURA	My friend and I named him Julian.
MIKE	Well, that was a nice name.

LAURA Thanks. We tried our best.

MIKE What did you do with him?

LAURA We went to the park, brushed him and cooked him eggs. Scrambled eggs were his favorite.

MIKE It sounds like you gave him a good life. If you need anything or just want to talk, all you need to do is ask me.

LAURA Thanks so much. I appreciate it. I will see how I feel later.

QUESTION TIME

Now answer these questions about the dialog.

1. What was Laura sad about?

2. How was today's Talking Tip used?

3. What was wrong with the dog?

4. What was the dog's name?

5. How would you help somebody in this situation?

TOPIC STORY

Read this story and talk about the most interesting things in the story.

Disrupting Rest in Peace

Tempers flared at Highland Acres Cemetery, here in New York, after the announcement the cemetery would close and relocate all the remains to another area. All of this is to make way for a new shopping mall.

"How dare they move the bodies of our loved ones!" said Seyeon June, a local resident whose father is buried at Highland Acres. "These aren't just statues or trees! These are the bodies of our mothers and fathers, grandfathers and grandmothers. This isn't a playground, it's a graveyard!"

Highland Acres Cemetery started making plans to move remains outside of the city limits in order to create space for commercial developers to begin construction on a new plaza of department stores, school and possibly an amusement park.

"We are trying to envision a brighter future for living residents and those to come," said Zach Burlon, owner of Swartout Developers Inc. "Those dead people are in the past. This shopping mall can be the future of the city. Plus, we're moving all those bodies anyway."

Swartout Developers promises to move the remains of people to a new location and create a new cemetery with similar design features and facilities as the old one. Swartout Developers repeated this chain of events in Eugene, Oregon as well as Boulder, Colorado. While this process isn't well liked, the end results are usually very positive.

"People generally aren't thrilled to learn the remains of their loved ones are being moved," said Bronson Weismann, who served as mayor of Boulder, Colorado during the time of that city's cemetery relocation project. "However, after everything is settled and they see the convenience and the tax revenue from the new shopping mall, most people will change their minds and settle down."

The Daily Catacombs Cemetery in Boulder closed in the year 2003. Soon after, Swartout began construction on the Kevin O'Brian Shopping Plaza, which opened in 2005. Experts estimate revenues from the mall to be about $3 billion a year. A portion of the tax money is reserved for the new Daily Catacombs Cemetery just outside of Boulder city limits. The other extra tax money goes towards education, the volunteer fire department and park management.

"I don't care about how much money our city will make," said June. "That doesn't make it right that they should disturb the final resting places of human beings! And just to make room for a shopping mall we don't need? When are we going to figure out that money isn't everything?"

Remains relocation may begin next July and should be completed within a year. After certain tests are passed, Swartout will start work on the shopping center. The construction company plans to finish within two years. Stores such as Target, Abercrombie & Fitch and Apple Computers all plan to move into the newly opened mall.

(Green Leaf Times-Newspaper: March 17, 2013)

COMPREHENSION QUESTIONS

Answer the following questions and write complete sentences.

1. Why is Seyeon June upset about the decision to relocate the remains at Highland Acres Cemetery?

____

2. What will replace the cemetery?

____

3. When will the construction begin and finish?

____

4. Where will the cemetery relocate to?

____

5. What are some of the positive outcomes from the proposed plan to relocate remains?

____

In a group, write and discuss what you think about funerals.

Would you want the bodies of your loved ones to be moved to another location? What type of funeral would you prefer? What are differences between funerals in the West and funerals in Korea?

____

____

____

____

____

HERE'S SOME MORE...

Read about culture from across the globe about today's topic.

Funeral Customs from around the World

Open or Closed?

In most countries the deceased body is placed into a casket made of wood, metal or other materials. The casket is placed in the front of the room where the funeral is being held. Most of time the casket is closed. However, one detail changes everything. Sometimes people want an "open casket funeral," which means the casket is open and people may view the corpse. There will be a line of people who will throw a flower or memento into the casket.

Ashes Away

Some people do not want to be buried, but cremated - which just means the body is burned to ashes. The ashes are then collected into an urn. While some people still bury the ashes and the urn, others wish their ashes to be spread in an ocean, a forest or other location the deceased person liked.

Wake Up!

In the past, people did not know how to check vital signs to see if somebody is dead. By accident, sometimes they buried people who were not dead, but just in a deep sleep, in a coma or just very drunk! So they started having events called "wakes" where everybody gathered around the body telling stories, drinking alcohol and singing. It was basically a party that lasted an entire night. Then if the person woke up, they celebrated. If the person stayed asleep, they assumed they were dead and buried them. Now a few people still use wakes as either a happy or sad occasion to trade stories and feelings about the person who passed away.

Bucket List

This phrase was made incredibly popular by the movie "Bucket List." However, creating these checklists gives many people an outlook at their goals. Some people write things they would like to accomplish such as to learn to play guitar, get married or earn a graduate school degree. Other folks like to write about places they would like to visit such as Mount Everest, Disneyland or the Amazon. What's on your bucket list?

(www.PointsInCase.com-Website: December 2010)

DYNAMITE DISCUSSION

Gather a group and discuss these following questions. When your group finishes, present your ideas to other students.

1. Would you want the graves of your family to be moved to make way for a new development? Why or why not? What if the development company or cemetery paid you?

2. What would you put on your Bucket List?

3. What type of funeral would you like? Big? Small? Indoors? Outdoors? Religious? Secular? Why?

4. Where would you like your funeral? In a church, funeral hall, a park or gymnasium? What landmarks or areas do you think are common for people to be buried?

5. Would you rather be cremated or buried? If cremated, where would you like your ashes spread? Who would you like to spread your ashes?

6. Name a celebrity death that affected you. Who was it? What did you do to mourn?

7. How would you react if a good friend asked you to attend their pet's funeral that was an hour away from your home on a Saturday? Would you go? Why or why not?

8. What are some good things about having a wake when people are happily telling stories about the deceased person? What could some bad things be?

9. What are some differences between funerals in Korea and the Western World?

10. What types of things would you say to console a friend who has just lost a loved one?

GET IT TOGETHER

Divide into two groups: one group the Pro team and the other the Con team. Write about the pros and cons of being cremated or buried. Then debate.

1. Would you be cremated or buried? Open or closed casket? Why?

____

____

2. What have people in your past done for their funerals? What did you think?

____

____

3. What are some pros of being buried or cremated? What are some cons?

Pros:

Cons:

Master

Lessons for Becoming a Great Conversationalist

Debate

Unit 3

Tattoo Taboos

UNIT 3

ICEBREAKERS

▷▷ Would you get a tattoo? Why or why not?

▷▷ How do you view friends, family, strangers or celebrities with tattoos?

▷▷ Why do you think people get tattoos?

RAPID FIRE

Brainstorm words or sentences related to tattoos.

	Words	Sentences
Noun	Ex) Tattoo, ink,	
Verb	Ex) To get worked on,	
Adjective	Ex) Painful,	

VOCABULARY PREVIEW

Fill in the blank with proper words using the following words.

Ban	Opponents	Convicts	Legislature
Popularity	Debase	Parlor	Stereotype

1. The government should ___________ tobacco advertising.
2. He went to the tattoo ___________ yesterday to get a tattoo.
3. People associate tattoos with mafia members or ___________.
4. Due to the ___________ of "Harry Potter" movies, the theater will open another showing.
5. The ___________ of the new same-sex marriage law gathered and protested outside City Hall.

IDIOM TIME! *Connect the idioms with their meanings.*

Learning idioms will help you sound more like a native speaker, but also, they're fun! Check out these idioms. What do they mean? When would you use them?

1. Getting inked	a. to appear dirty
2. A carnival freakshow	b. something that hurts a lot or to be in a lot of trouble
3. Something the cat dragged in	c. to receive a tattoo
4. Have guts	d. be brave
5. To be skinned alive	e. somebody with multiple tattoos

Write three sentences with any of the idioms we learned about today.

1. ____

2. ____

3. ____

CONVERSATION

TALKING TIPS

These skills will make you a better English speaker and listener. Pay attention!

Arguing With Friends

When making an argument, sometimes you will need to agree to disagree. This means you can both keep your own differing opinions while still maintaining a friendship and not offending each other. One thing you can say is "I see your point, but I'm going to stick with my own thinking." Or you can say, "I understand your side of thinking. Can you give me more reasons or examples to believe your side?" You can use this when debating with a friend. Neither side wants to give in to the other, but you don't want to end a friendship over a difference of opinion.

TALKING TIME

Practice this couple's conversation about tattoos using Talking Tips.

OAKLAND I hate tattoos. They make people look dirty and weird.

MELISSA I don't know. Sometimes I think they look pretty cool.

OAKLAND Who wants to have all that writing on your body?

MELISSA Maybe they are just trying to express themselves or remember something important.

OAKLAND If something is so important, why would you need a permanent tattoo as a reminder?

MELISSA I don't know about that. I won basketball awards and trophies in high school, and I still keep them around my house. Even though I remember them all of the time, it is still nice to be able to show them off when other people come to my home.

OAKLAND Well, what happens when you get older and your skin starts to sag or get all stretchy? Or what happens when that ink begins to fade or if you have an accident?

MELISSA Oh come on. My grandfather has a tattoo on his arm from the war and he is still proud of it. I am sure it isn't as pretty as it used to be, but he still enjoys showing it off and telling us stories.

OAKLAND Okay, I see your point, but I think a war tattoo is a lot different than getting your boyfriend's or girlfriend's name tattooed. But I still think they should be outlawed to keep our people looking prim and proper.

MELISSA Alright, I see your point with the part about war tattoos versus name tattoos, but, I still think tattoos are a choice. You don't have to get one, but if other people want to do it, why don't we just let them?

OAKLAND Well I guess we'll just have to agree to disagree.

QUESTION TIME

Now answer these questions about the dialog.

1. Why did Oakland and Melissa disagree?

2. How did they use today's Talking Tip?

3. What did you think about their arguments?

4. Why did Melissa's grandfather have a tattoo?

5. Who do you agree with? Why?

TOPIC STORY

Read this story and talk about the most interesting things in the story.

Tattoo Taboos

Yesterday the Korean legislature debated whether or not to ban tattoo parlors on the peninsula. Supporters of the proposed law argued that tattoos make people look "trashy, dirty and like something the cat dragged in." However, opponents of the possible legislation disagreed and said tattoos are a manner of personal expression and fashion.

"We don't want Korea's youth to look like gangsters or prisoners. Only gangsters and prisoners defile their bodies with tattoos. Not only do these tattoo parlors debase our children, but they are also dens of debauchery such as drinking and drugs," said Lee Hang-rok of the Conservative Party.

The Conservative Party's main worry is that tattoos will explode with popularity like in the United States. According to some studies, about 25 percent of Americans from the ages of 18 to 30 sport at least one tattoo. Koreans have long associated tattoos with mafia members or convicts.

"We believe our young people should appear to be proud and beautiful, not trashy, dirty and like something the cat dragged in," said Lee at a press conference after the debate. "Why would somebody want to look like a carnival freakshow?"

On the other side of the fence, the Liberal Party of Korea wants to let people be freer with their bodies. "Who cares what people do to their bodies? We allow our children to receive more plastic surgery per capita than any other country in the world," said Ahn Tae-ik. "Why don't we let them get tattoos if they want? We are a free country, therefore we should allow our children to be free."

Some people claim tattoos are lower class, while others mention that famous world celebrities such as David Beckham, Johnny Depp and Angelina Jolie wear tattoos. While the trend isn't as popular with celebrities in Korea, some K-Pop stars and drama actors are starting to ink their bodies a little more than in the past. The Conservative Party worries that if famous people start with tattoos, some adolescents will follow.

"I think this whole thing is ridiculous," said Jung Sae-young, a tattooist at Dark Side Tattoo Parlor in Hongdae. "The Conservatives claim we are dirty and disgusting people for helping people decorate their bodies. Come to my shop any time and see how clean and orderly we are. I bet my shop is cleaner than most doctors' offices. I use new and clean needles every time I start a tattoo. My inks are high quality and I have never been to prison or joined some kind of gang."

A large proportion of Koreans believe only gangsters and convicts tattoo their bodies. Many Americans also held this belief. In addition, Americans also linked tattoos with biker gangs. However, when many US military men returned from World War II with tattoos, that stereotype started to break.

Tattoos certainly aren't common in the American office or corporate workplace, but they are becoming more accepted as the next generation joins the workforce.

"This is just another trend that Koreans need to deal with, just like allowing men to grow their hair longer, wear different colors like pink or wear shorts," said Ahn. "We need to quit being such a stuffy society and just let people be themselves. Also, this will help our nation and our people to quit judging people from their outside appearances. Who cares what somebody looks like as long as they can do their job?"

On the other hand, the Conservative Party is fully supporting the tattoo ban. "Our youth and our people represent our country and our culture. Do we really want the rest of the world to look at us like we are criminals or members of a rock band? Absolutely not," said Lee.

While much more debate will take place, the vote for the law will be next Thursday.

(Yatap Yelp- Newspaper: March 24, 2012)

COMPREHENSION QUESTIONS

Answer the following questions and write complete sentences.

1. What law are Korean Conservatives trying to pass?

2. Find one reason why the Liberal Party wants to allow tattoos.

3. How did the tattoo artist defend his profession?

4. Who did Koreans, and Americans, believe were the only people who received tattoos?

5. Which group changed Americans' perception of tattoos?

In a group, write and discuss what you think about the tattoo ban.

Should they allow or restrict tattoos? What should the age requirement be? How do you view people with tattoos?

HERE'S SOME MORE...

Read about culture from across the globe about today's topic.

Tattoo Tips

Tattoos may be becoming more commonplace, but there are still some misconceptions about them. Here are some tips for asking about tattoos and getting a tattoo.

Asking about Ink

Tattoos are growing with popularity, but even though not everybody may have them, most people like to see them. In some situations, asking to view somebody's tattoos may be either rude or inconvenient, such as at a formal meeting or when children are present. Other times, the tattoo may be in an inappropriate place, or feature improper artwork. So try to keep these things in mind.

Getting Ink Done

Tattoos can take only a few minutes or a lot of hours. Either or, if you get a tattoo, you will live with it for your entire life. Here is some advice when getting a tattoo:

A. Think about your tattoo idea long and hard. Remember, you can always get a tattoo, but you cannot always remove it.

B. Consider the placement of your tattoo. If the spot you choose to get inked is easy to see, most people will know you have a tattoo. They may draw a conclusion on you. "Never get a tattoo a judge can see," says Nick Claxton, owner of Rooster & Moon Coffee Shop in Denver, Colorado. "Because they will certainly judge you, and not always in the good way."

C. Is your art design something trendy? Stop and consider if this tattoo will still be cool in six months, or six years.

D. If you are going to tattoo the name of a significant other, lover, wife or husband, be sure this person will be in your life forever. If not, maybe think of getting a bracelet or necklace that is decorated with each other's names.

E. Tattoos hurt. Depending on where your tattoo artist starts drilling the needle, you could be in some pain or a lot of pain. Arm and legs are usually popular because they do not hurt as much. The feet and the spinal area allegedly scream with agony when being tattooed. Tattoos take some time and money, but they also take guts!

(www.TattooTipsFromHays.com-Website: January 2008)

DYNAMITE DISCUSSION

Gather a group and discuss these following questions. When your group finishes, present your ideas to other students.

1. Do you think Korea should outlaw tattoos? Why or why not?

2. Would you get a tattoo? Why? What would you get tattooed? Where would you get it on your body?

3. Where would you go to get a tattoo done? Would you go to a tattoo parlor? Would you go to a friend who had a tattoo gun?

4. How do you view people with tattoos? Do you respect or disrespect them? Do you treat them differently? Why?

5. Name some celebrities with tattoos. What do you think of them?

6. Why do you think so many celebrities tattoo themselves?

7. Some tattoo parlors enact a waiting period so the client can be positive the tattoo is really wanted and not a mistake. What other rules could be started in order to make sure people make the right decisions?

8. What are some differences between views about tattoos in Korea or the Western World?

9. What do different tattoos mean? What does a cross mean? A dragon? YOLO?

10. If you got a tattoo, would you hide it from your parents? How?

GET IT TOGETHER

Divide into two groups: one group the Pro team and the other the Con team. Write about the pros and cons of wearing tattoos. Then debate.

1. Would you get a tattoo? Why or why not?

____

____

2. What do you think about friends, family, strangers or celebrities with tattoos?

____

____

3. What are some pros of having tattoos? What are some cons of tattoos?

Pros:

Cons:

M a s t e r

Lessons for Becoming a Great Conversationalist

D e b a t e

Master

Lessons for Becoming a Great Conversationalist

Debate

Unit 4

That's Not So Bully

UNIT 4

ICEBREAKERS

- Is bullying in schools, the military or on the streets a big problem in Korea? Why or why not?
- Was bullying a problem in your elementary school, middle school or high school? How?
- What can be done to stop bullying?

RAPID FIRE

Brainstorm words or sentences related to bullies.

	Words	Sentences
Noun	Ex) Bully, schoolyard,	
Verb	Ex) To get picked on,	
Adjective	Ex) Different,	

VOCABULARY PREVIEW

Fill in the blank with proper words using the following words.

Disruptive	Clasp	Twerps	Plethora
Podium	Coddled	Offensive	Bigotry

1. The angry teacher called his students "Annoying ___________."
2. The ___________ noise came from the construction going on next door to my apartment, which was annoying because I was working on my homework.
3. Some mothers make sure their babies are ___________ all the time.
4. Since I have so many, would you say I have a ___________ of piñatas?
5. Try not to use ___________ words when speaking to your grandparents.

IDIOM TIME! Connect the idioms with their meanings.

Learning idioms will help you sound more like a native speaker, but also, they're fun! Check out these idioms. What do they mean? When would you use them?

1. Out of this world	a. get married
2. Tie the knot	b. bullied
3. Bat in the cave	c. very odd, interesting or stupid
4. Picked on	d. having a booger or mucus in your nose
5. Like clockwork	e. working perfectly

Write three sentences with any of the idioms we learned about today.

1. ____

2. ____

3. ____

CONVERSATION

TALKING TIPS

These skills will make you a better English speaker and listener. Pay attention!

Using Your Body To Speak

What are you supposed to do with your hands during a speech? First off, what should you NOT do with your hands? Putting your hands in your pockets, clicking a pen or picking your nose or ears are incredibly distracting and disruptive. So don't do it!

Some people will tell you to place your hands on the podium or desk, but what happens when there isn't any place to put your hands? Some will tell you to clasp your hands in front of you, but that can make your speech boring.

A good thing to try is called "talking with your hands." Talking with your hands is a skill people learn when giving public speeches.

This can be as easy as showing your crowd one finger when you say something such as "the first thing you should look at when looking at cars." Or you could show one finger for when you say, "One time I went to band camp."

Think about how many symbols or things you can do with your hands. There are peace signs, thumbs up or down, A-OK and a finger circling your ear to symbolize "crazy." Try to incorporate these into your speaking.

One thing to remember is: don't use your hands too much. If your hands are moving all over the place during your speech, people can be really distracted or focus more on your hands than the words you are saying.

SKILL BUILDER :

Read this short speech and look at the underlined words. What types of hand gestures could you make while making a presentation using this speech in front of a crowd?

Hello everyone. My name is Stan. Today I would like to talk about my favorite movie "The Avengers." I saw "Avengers" six times in the movie theater. This movie was so fun to watch and went perfectly with popcorn.

My first favorite Avenger is Iron Man, also known as Tony Stark. He is really smart, handsome and funny. He wears an armored suit that allows him to fly, makes him bulletproof and he can shoot lasers from his hands. The second best Avenger is the Hulk. He is big and green and mean! He was a scientist who had a big accident and now his power is going crazy and crushing things with his big muscles. Thor is probably the third coolest. I don't know that much about him except that he carries a big hammer and has long, beautiful hair. Captain America is probably the most boring Avenger. He carries a shield and knows a lot about leadership, but everybody was way more interesting than him.

I am very excited for the next "Avengers" movie. I even started reading some of the comic books and those are sometimes even better than the movie. Plus, you learn more about the characters! How cool! Okay, now it is time for me to end my speech. Thank you for listening to my presentation.

QUESTION TIME

Now answer these questions about the speech.

1. What is Stan's speech about?
2. Who is Stan's favorite Avenger? Why?
3. How do you think Stan used his hands during the speech?
4. What else has Stan done to learn about the characters from "The Avengers?"
5. What type of speech would you write about your favorite movie? How would you use your hands?

TOPIC STORY

Read this story and talk about the most interesting things in the story.

That's Not So Bully

While some people hate CCTV, the usage of CCTV in schools proved to be incredibly helpful in Grandport, England. Now middle school students being bullied by others can tell a principal, teacher or other school faculty member about the abuse they received. Then the school employee can find the incident on the recorded tapes and the students can point to the bully who picked on them.

"This new system seemed to greatly reduce the bullying in our school this year," said Eliot McKinney, the vice principal at Grandport Middle School (GMS). "Our cameras are catching bullies in the act, therefore allowing the faculty to punish and expel these punks who roam our halls and terrorize our students."

At GMS, if a bully is caught verbally or physically abusing another student, the bully is sent to a special class on two weekends about why ridiculing, hitting or threatening others is wrong. "This is keeping our students safe, as well as teaching others that being mean is wrong," said McKinney.

Unfortunately, not everybody is happy about this new program. "I got in huge trouble because I was just joking with my friends," said Mikey Black, a 15-year-old student punished for bullying at GMS. "All I did was call my friend some names and pretend to almost punch him and then I got in trouble and needed to take this stupid class. It's out of this world! What a waste of time."

Even some parents are protesting the CCTV. "I understand the need to stop bullying in our schools. But to videotape everything our children do? That's ridiculous," said Sandy Schmidt, a parent of two GMS children. "And kids aren't as stupid as we think. If they're going to bully somebody, they'll find out where there aren't cameras and just do it there. There are still going to be fights in the physical education locker rooms."

GMS was made internationally famous last year when a YouTube video surfaced of a child getting a "swirly" in the boys' restroom. A "swirly" is when one or more students hold a victim by the feet and dip the victim's head into a toilet, then flush. The responses to the video came from across the globe and varied. Here are some examples of comments:

"How horrifying! I've never heard or seen such a thing. What is wrong with youngsters today?"

"That's a fact of life, and kids should just learn to deal with it instead of being coddled little wimps."

"These twerps should be sent to boot camp or prison. Whichever comes first."

"I was picked on as a kid. It helped me grow up to be the person I am today. I raised my children right, so they will never do this, or have this kind of thing done to them."

There is talk about perhaps putting cameras in physical education locker rooms, as well as bathrooms. Again, there is much debate about this.

"These are children. Do we really need to watch them go to the toilet or shower while they are at school?" said Schmidt.

"If these measures stop one instance of bullying, they are worth it," said McKinney.

The Grandport Educational Board will vote on CCTV in private areas next quarter.

(The Chronicle- Newspaper: August 24, 2011)

COMPREHENSION QUESTIONS

Answer the following questions and write complete sentences.

1. What is Grandport Middle School using CCTV to catch?

2. Why is Sandy Schmidt mad at this usage?

3. What did Mikey Black say was a problem with the CCTV policy in his school?

4. What incident made GMS famous worldwide?

5. Where is the next spot GMS may put CCTV?

In a group, write and discuss what you think about bullies and bullying.

HERE'S SOME MORE...

Read about culture from across the globe about today's topic.

That's Not So Gay and That's Not So Retarded

Over the years, calling somebody or something "gay" or "retarded" became popular slang for some English-speaking youths around the world. If a man sees a boy wearing a pink shirt, he might say "You're wearing a pink shirt. That's so gay." Another example is a person may fail a test and say, "I feel so retarded right now."

While these words are not technically swearing, they are offensive to many different people, and it doesn't matter if they are gay or retarded. However the preferred words to describe somebody who is gay is "homosexual" and the preferred words to describe somebody who is retarded is either "mentally disabled," "mentally handicapped," "special" or simply "slow."

"English is a language with a plethora of different words. Why do we need to call others 'gay' or 'retarded?'" asks Pearl Davenport, an advocate for Stop Discrimination NOW, an Auckland, Australia-based group that fights to create equality and eliminate bigotry, racism and violence against others. "Seriously, why don't you just call somebody 'weird' or 'stupid' or any number of other insults?"

Stop Discrimination NOW is attempting to remove these words from the everyday speaking in hopes that people will one day consider them just as offensive as other racial slurs or terms commonly used in the past.

(Colorado Daily- Newspaper: July 7, 2013)

DYNAMITE DISCUSSION

Gather a group and discuss these following questions. When your group finishes, present your ideas to other students.

1. What do you think of using CCTV to catch bullies? Did they use it in your school?

2. Were you or anybody else bullied in school? What happened?

3. Why are some students bullied and why do others become bullies?

4. What are other ways to stop bullying?

5. Who is bullied more, boys or girls? Why do you think so?

6. When do you think people are bullied the most? In elementary school, middle school, high school, university, the military, the workplace or any other place? Why are they bullied so much in that time?

7. Do you agree with the removal of "gay" or "retarded" as insults? Why or why not?

8. What are some English terms or phrases you find offensive? What are they?

9. Are there any words in Korean that you wish people wouldn't use any more? What are they?

10. How can eliminating these words help prevent discrimination?

GET IT TOGETHER

Divide into two groups: one group the Pro team and the other the Con team. Write about the pros and cons of catching bullies. Then debate.

1. What types of bullying did you see growing up?

____

____

2. How can bullied children be harmed mentally, physically or socially?

____

____

3. What are some pros of CCTV? What are some cons?

Pros:

Cons:

M a s t e r

Lessons for Becoming a Great Conversationalist

D e b a t e

Master

Lessons for Becoming a Great Conversationalist

Debate

Unit 5

Varying Vices

UNIT 5

ICEBREAKERS

- If you smoke, when did you and your friends start smoking?
- Do you think too many people in Korea smoke? Why or why not?
- What are some other gross habits people do?

RAPID FIRE

Brainstorm words or sentences related to smoking.

	Words	Sentences
Noun	Ex) Habits, tobacco,	
Verb	Ex) To smoke,	
Adjective	Ex) Unhealthy,	

VOCABULARY PREVIEW

Fill in the blank with proper words using the following words.

Varying	Outrage	Mandatory	Insist
Vices	Advocate	Emitting	Prevails

1. He needs to take the ___________ driving class if he wants to get his driver's license.
2. I think it is an ___________ that my cable company charged me extra for channels I don't even get.
3. I joined UNICEF because I want to be an ___________ for freedom.
4. The factory is in trouble for ___________ so much pollution.
5. I wonder why so many celebrities have so many drinking problems, drug addictions and other ___________.

IDIOM TIME! *Connect the idioms with their meanings.*

Learning idioms will help you sound more like a native speaker, but also, they're fun! Check out these idioms. What do they mean? When would you use them?

1. Break into (something)	a. feeling sad
2. Down in the dumps	b. enter a new professional field or scene
3. Preaching to the choir	c. incredibly fat
4. Going viral	d. speaking about something that people already believe in
5. Weigh a ton	e. spreading quickly

Write three sentences with any of the idioms we learned about today.

1. ______________________________

2. ______________________________

3. ______________________________

CONVERSATION

TALKING TIPS

These skills will make you a better English speaker and listener. Pay attention!

"Are You Going?" Or "Will You Go?"

Two popular phrases in English are "Are you going to..." and "I'm going to..." This can be difficult for new English speakers to get used to, but also incredibly useful once a person gets the hang of it. Often, "Are you going to..." and "I'm going to..." are used with infinitives forms of verbs such as: "to swim," "to bike," "to eat pasta" or "to watch a movie." So you would say, "Are you going to write a novel?" "No, I'm going to play computer games." These phrases can also mean traveling to a place, such as, "Are you going to James' house?" "No, I'm going to the gym."

TALKING TIME

Practice this couple's conversation about tobacco using Talking Tips.

CONSTANCE Boy, your room is dirty! What are all these half-full Coke cans doing here? I am kind of thirsty...

MELVIN Oh, don't drink those! Those are filled with spit!

CONSTANCE Gross! Why are you spitting in Coke cans?

MELVIN I chew tobacco, and I spit in cans. I know it sounds gross, but at least I don't smoke.

CONSTANCE That is so gross. Are you ever going to quit?

MELVIN Why should I quit? I don't smoke. Chewing relaxes me after a hard day of work and I only do it a little bit.

CONSTANCE	But maybe you are going to get half your face chopped off like those people on the news. That sure wouldn't be relaxing!
MELVIN	I can tell by the way that you're staring at me that you're angry. But this is something I am going to do. I don't think it is a huge problem right now.
CONSTANCE	I don't even want to look at you right now. Think about how bad tobacco is for your health though.
MELVIN	Yes, it probably is, but it keeps me going during a hard day. What is worse, being lazy or indulging myself a little bit once in a while?
CONSTANCE	Okay, I guess I see your point. I am still going to disagree though.
MELVIN	That's just your opinion.

QUESTION TIME

Now answer these questions about the dialog.

1. Why does Melvin spit into Coke cans?

2. What is Constance worried about will happen to Melvin if he keeps doing what he's doing?

3. How did they use today's Talking Tip?

4. What are Melvin's reasons for using tobacco?

5. Who do you agree with?

TOPIC STORY

Read this story and talk about the most interesting things in the story.

Varying Vices

Parent and health groups are furious that tobacco companies are starting to market chewing tobacco or "dipping tobacco" to Koreans. Commonly known as "chew" or "dip," this type of tobacco looks like cigarette tobacco. However, the dip is inserted into the lower lip or cheek instead of smoked.

"This is an outrage. We are already dealing with the hundreds of thousands, maybe even millions of people who smoke in Korea. Now we need to deal with another type of tobacco," said Leonard Moy an anti-smoking advocate from the University of Bravo in Taepyung, Korea.

Eco-Localizer, an anti-smoking group, performed a survey and found out that about 50 percent of Korean men claim to be smokers, while about four percent of women smoke in this country. The findings also discovered more men smoke than women because many males start smoking during the two-year mandatory military service that Koreans need to serve.

Chewing tobacco is popular in the United States and some areas of Europe such as Sweden. Instead of emitting smoke, the "chewer" or "dipper" spits out the tobacco juice, either on the ground or into a container, commonly called a "spittoon."

"No matter if Koreans chew or smoke tobacco, it isn't good for them," said Moy. "Should we ask our children and family members to use heroin instead of drinking alcohol? Switching one problem to another doesn't help anything or anybody."

Since Koreans smoke so much, American tobacco companies are attempting to break into the large market for tobacco. "We saw a giant change of tobacco use in Koreans from the 1960s to now," said Jason Pilot, president of Planet Easton Smokeless Tobacco. "Back then, most Koreans smoked pipes, but now we are seeing Koreans almost only smoke cigarettes. We are going to try and change Koreans' habits again by getting them to switch to dip or chew."

Pilot continued to discuss other benefits of chewing tobacco. "You don't see as much litter or pollution with chew. Smokers throw cigarette butts everywhere and smoke goes everywhere else," said the tobacco president. "However the refuse my clients make is absolutely minimal. It's just some spit that we keep to ourselves and some tobacco leaves that we throw away. Or birds eat it. Virtually no mess."

According to the Korean Herald, smoking is the highest cause of death in Korea, with about 40,000 a year. "Our hospitals are overflowing with people who have lung diseases because of smoking. Now they will be bursting with even more people with lip and mouth diseases because of chewing tobacco," said Moy. "I'm asking everybody to do a Google-Search of the horrible things both smoking and chewing can do to your body, lungs, mouth, teeth, skin and other family members. Just please quit."

(Busan Sun-Newspaper: July 9, 2013)

COMPREHENSION QUESTIONS

Answer the following questions and write complete sentences.

1. How is dipping tobacco different from smoking?

____

2. Why does Leonard Moy insist that dipping tobacco is just as bad as smoking?

____

3. Why does Jason Pilot insist that dipping is better than smoking?

____

4. What types of health problems does dipping tobacco start?

____

5. What percentage of Korean men smoke? How many die from smoking?

____

In a group, write and discuss what you think about tobacco.

Write your opinion of tobacco of any type. Should we ban this substance or make it more difficult to get? Why do people start smoking? What do you think about smoking in public places such as cafes or restaurants? How do you view smokers?

____

____

____

____

____

HERE'S SOME MORE...

Read about culture from across the globe about today's topic.

A Potentially Dangerous Diet

Hundreds of years ago, the Native Americans discovered something good about tobacco, and that knowledge still prevails. Nicotine, the active ingredient in cigarettes and chewing tobacco is an appetite suppressant. This means you feel less hungry after a nicotine buzz.

In the early 1900s in the USA, tobacco companies caught onto this thinking and told women that smoking would make them thin. Now a dietician who is also a personal trainer is telling her clients to either start smoking or chewing tobacco.

"Tobacco is a natural substance that helps people not to feel starved to death while dieting," said Tera Benson, from Waist Management, a personal training company in Roget, North Carolina. "And tobacco is actually safer than some of these other diet products out there."

"The Dipping Diet" (as it has been called) shows a lot of results with former clients. About 40 percent of people under Benson's program lose weight and keep it off. Granted, some of them start smoking as well, but most are happy with the outcome. "I used to weigh a ton, but when I started taking a dip whenever I felt hungry I started to lose weight like crazy," said Randy Hogan, a coffee shop owner in Cincinnati. "What is better, using tobacco or being grossly overweight? My new girlfriend will answer that for you!"

(Health-Magazine: October 2009)

DYNAMITE DISCUSSION

Gather a group and discuss these following questions. When your group finishes, present your ideas to other students.

1. What would you say to a friend whom you want to stop using tobacco?

2. Both are bad for your health. What do you think is worse: chewing tobacco or smoking? Why?

3. Why do you think Koreans smoke so much?

4. At what age do most Koreans start smoking? When do they quit smoking? How do they do it?

5. What is more worse: being lazy or indulging in a bad habit like smoking once in a while?

6. Besides smoking, what are other giant health problems in Korea?

7. What are some differences between views about smoking in Korea or the Western World?

8. If you could choose being fat or being addicted to tobacco, which would you choose? Why?

9. What are other ways people can become healthy or lose weight besides using tobacco?

10. Can you think of other bad habits people start? What are they? Why do they start?

GET IT TOGETHER

Divide into two groups: one group the Pro team and the other the Con team. Write about the pros and cons of smoking or dipping tobacco. Then debate.

1. Why do you think so many Koreans smoke? Do many students smoke? Why or why not?

____

____

2. Do you think smoking looks cool? Dirty? How have views on smoking changed in the past few years?

____

____

3. What are some pros of smoking? What are some cons of smoking?

Pros:

Cons:

M a s t e r

Lessons for Becoming a Great Conversationalist

D e b a t e

M a s t e r

Lessons for Becoming a Great Conversationalist

D e b a t e

Unit 6

Open Doors for Drunk Drivers

UNIT 6

ICEBREAKERS

- What should the punishment for drunk driving be? Why?
- What is your opinion about people after they have been arrested for driving drunk?
- What are some pros of punishing drunk drivers for the rest of their lives? What are some cons of punishing drunk drivers for the rest of their lives?

RAPID FIRE

Brainstorm words or sentences related to drinking and driving.

	Words	Sentences
Noun	Ex) Alcohol, driver,	
Verb	Ex) To arrest,	
Adjective	Ex) Troublesome,	

VOCABULARY PREVIEW

Fill in the blank with proper words using the following words.

Taboo	Ignited	Grace period	Intersection
Rush	Violations	Discredit	Motorists

1. The new road map helps __________ find the correct route to take.
2. She __________ a cigarette after her job interview.
3. If you drive past that __________ you will see the street you are looking for.
4. After we removed our basketball jerseys during our game, our team was punished, fined and suspended because the referee said we had too many uniform __________.
5. Cheating is a __________ to all your ancestors.

IDIOM TIME! *Connect the idioms with their meanings.*

Learning idioms will help you sound more like a native speaker, but also, they're fun! Check out these idioms. What do they mean? When would you use them?

1. Opening doors	a. to start something fresh
2. An albatross around the neck	b. to be punished for something
3. Turn over a new leaf	c. giving opportunities
4. Behind bars	d. a mark of shame for a past mistake
5. Raked over the coals	e. in jail

Write three sentences with any of the idioms we learned about today.

1. ____________________

2. ____________________

3. ____________________

CONVERSATION

TALKING TIPS

These skills will make you a better English speaker and listener. Pay attention!

I'm Sorry, That's Personal

A taboo is something that is forbidden. Personal information is something that some people may be uncomfortable conversing about. All countries and people have different views of what is taboo or what is personal.

If you are curious about one of these topics, just say, "Can I ask... / Is it okay to ask... / Would you mind talking about...?" If the person does not feel comfortable discussing the topic, they can just answer, "No. That's personal." If the person feels fine, carry on your conversation!

TALKING TIME

Practice this couple's conversation about driving using Talking Tips.

NATE Ah shucks. I was speeding yesterday and a police officer gave me a ticket. Can I ask, have you ever received a ticket before?

CANDY Of course you can ask! I once got a ticket for running a stop light. I was just in a rush.

NATE Oh wow. Now I don't feel so bad.

CANDY Now it's my turn. Would you mind talking about if you've ever been in a car accident?

NATE No problem. A few years ago my mom lost control and crashed into a parked car. We were almost killed.

CANDY Oh gosh. How terrible!

NATE Yeah, it was scary. We tried avoiding a drunk driver. Luckily, we did, but unfortunately we still crashed. That's why I feel like drunk drivers should be raked over the coals.

CANDY That is such a big problem now.

NATE Yes it is. Is it okay to ask if you've ever driven drunk?

CANDY No. That's personal.

NATE Why? Because you've done it before?

CANDY Maybe in the past, but I have changed my ways.

QUESTION TIME

Now answer these questions about the dialog.

1. What did Candy and Nate discuss?

2. How did they use today's Talking Tip?

3. How did Nate almost die?

4. What does Nate think the penalty for drunk driving should be? What do you think?

5. Do you think this was a polite conversation? Why?

TOPIC STORY

Read this story and talk about the most interesting things in the story.

Opening Doors for Drunk Drivers

Should foreigners with bad pasts be allowed to work in the Republic of Korea? This is the topic being raised by a group called Advancement for Wayguk Rights (AWR), an organization that pushes for better treatment of foreigners in Korea. AWR wants to change the rule so more foreigners are allowed to come into the country to work as teachers, engineers or other jobs. This hot-button issue ignited a debate this week.

"Everybody has done something stupid in their past," said Rich Levi, the spokesperson of AWR and the head teacher at Best Kids Academy in Bucheon. "If somebody wants to enter this country, but has had a flaw in their record, but learned their lesson, why don't we forgive them and allow them to teach here?"

Levi and his group are trying to allow foreigners with past violations to turn over a new leaf. Their proposition is that if a person received a Driving Under the Influence of Alcohol Violation (DUI), then the offender should stay clean for five years. After this five-year grace period, this person should be allowed to enter the country instead of being banned for life.

Not everybody feels the same way. "Driving drunk is careless, stupid and dangerous. Do we really want to be inviting careless, stupid and dangerous people into our country," said Inhang Kim, a government worker who fights for even stricter immigration laws. "Do we really want these ex-criminals coming in and taking our jobs?"

According to the United States Center for Disease Control, somebody is arrested for drunk driving every 48 minutes in the USA. That amounts to about 1.4 million people a year. Korea restricts admission to the country for foreigners with tickets for a DUI. If a foreigner already works in Korea, but receives a DUI in another country, that foreigner can be fired instantly as well as deported from Korea.

AWR feels this action is too extreme. "We all know DUIs are serious. But should violators have an albatross tied around their necks for the rest of their lives?" asked Levi. "I don't think so. We all know people grow more mature as they age. I don't think someone should be punished for the rest of their lives for something they did so long ago."

(Bucheon Daily- Newspaper: December 24, 2013)

COMPREHENSION QUESTIONS

Answer the following questions and write complete sentences.

1. What law does AWR want to change?

2. How does AWR want to change this rule?

3. How often does somebody get arrested for drunken driving in the USA?

4. What is the punishment for a foreigner who is arrested for a DUI in Korea?

5. How does Inhang Kim feel about this possible change?

In a group, write and discuss what you think about the drinking and driving.

Should Korea allow foreign teachers, engineers or doctors into the country if these foreigners violated laws such as Driving Under the Influence of alcohol? Why? How long should the grace period be? What do you think about drunk drivers?

HERE'S SOME MORE...

Read about culture from across the globe about today's topic.

Say 'Cheese!'

If you run a red light in some neighborhoods, prepare for the Department of Motor Vehicles to send a photo of you driving in your car to your mailbox. Attached to that photo will be at least a $150 fine. Cities across the world are putting highly intelligent cameras that sense when a driver runs a red light or speeds through an intersection.

Government workers prefer this method because the cameras are cheaper than posting police officers everywhere. The cameras never need time off for vacations or sick days. However, the devices do need to be maintained. "These cameras are not a discredit to our women and men in the police force," said Brooke Ariel, the mayor of Atlanta, Georgia. "However, these cameras are saving and earning a ton of money for local governments."

As of now, the governments using the intersection cameras' photos as "undeniable evidence," which means nobody can argue with officials whether or not they ran a stoplight. This brings up problems with drivers because they say sometimes the roads are slippery or icy. Motorists say if they slam on the brakes they could get into an accident, so sometimes running the light is safer than braking immediately.

(Atlanta Weekly- Newspaper: September 1, 2012)

DYNAMITE DISCUSSION

Gather a group and discuss these following questions. When your group finishes, present your ideas to other students.

1. Do you think Korea should allow ex-criminals into the country? Why or why not?

2. What should the penalty for drinking and driving be? How long should the penalty last?

3. Do you believe in the phrase "forgive and forget?" Why or why not?

4. How do you view people who received DUIs? How about people who were punished for other bad crimes? Why?

5. Why do you think so many people in the USA are arrested for DUIs?

6. What are some ways to prevent drinking and driving?

7. How do you feel about intersection cameras? Do you think they are helpful? What about icy roads and the cameras?

8. Who is arrested more, men or women? People from which country? What types of crimes are the most serious?

9. Have you ever been in a car accident? What happened?

10. Where do people drink and drive the most, in the country or in the city? Why?

GET IT TOGETHER

Divide into two groups: one group the Pro team and the other the Con teams. Write about the pros and cons of drunk-driving punishments. Then debate.

1. What do you think the punishment for drinking and driving should be? Why?

____

____

2. Does Korea need foreign workers so badly that they should allow some with criminal pasts? Why do you think so?

____

____

3. What are some pros of restricting foreigners because of criminal records? What are some cons?

Pros:

Cons:

M a s t e r

Lessons for Becoming a Great Conversationalist

D e b a t e

Master

Lessons for Becoming a Great Conversationalist

Debate

Unit 7

Waiter, There Aren't Flies in My Soup

UNIT 7

ICEBREAKERS

- Do you eat bundeggi? Do you like it?
- What are some weird foods that you have eaten? Where were you?
- Do you judge a culture by the things they eat? Why?

RAPID FIRE

Brainstorm words or sentences related to eating bugs.

	Words	Sentences
Noun	Ex) Food, snacks,	
Verb	Ex) To eat,	
Adjective	Ex) Delicious,	

VOCABULARY PREVIEW

Fill in the blank with proper words using the following words.

Engaging	Colossal	Entomophagy	Vendors
Status	Dietician	Connoisseurs	Disrespect

1. The garbage became a __________ pile because nobody took it out for five days.
2. The best professors are __________ with students.
3. I like to watch television programs where chefs and __________ test out different foods.
4. Sometimes people become sick when they buy food from street __________.
5. Other countries practice __________, but many Western countries are picky about what they eat.

IDIOM TIME! *Connect the idioms with their meanings.*

Learning idioms will help you sound more like a native speaker, but also, they're fun! Check out these idioms. What do they mean? When would you use them?

1. Roll the dice	a. take a chance
2. Give it a shot	b. secrets
3. Kill two birds with one stone	c. very surprising
4. Knock your socks off	d. finishing multiple things with minimal effort
5. Skeletons in the closet	e. to try something new

Write three sentences with any of the idioms we learned about today.

1. ______________________________

2. ______________________________

3. ______________________________

CONVERSATION

TALKING TIPS

These skills will make you a better English speaker and listener. Pay attention!

Let Your Eyes Do Some Talking

A big problem facing many Koreans who are learning English is eye contact. Usually, Westerners try to make eye contact with the person they speak to during a conversation. This is not a sign of disrespect in the West.

Eye contact helps create a more engaging conversation and can make the other person believe you are listening to them. Looking somebody in the eyes is a sign of connecting with somebody.

Practice looking people in the eyes when you speak with others, no matter their age or status. This may feel awkward if you have never done this before, but it can be a colossal help to your conversation skills.

Remember, this isn't a staring contest. You are allowed to look away and blink. When speaking in front of a small-to-medium-sized group, try to look at everybody in the room for a few seconds. Make a circle or a pattern out of eye contact.

If you are nervous with big public speeches, here's a tip. When speaking to a massive group, pick only a few people and make eye contact with them. Make sure they are spread out in the room. This way you appear to be speaking to everybody in the area, but really you only need to trouble yourself with a few people.

Some people say, "The eyes are the window to a person's soul." Your eyes can do a lot of talking. You don't need to stare or glare at somebody. Squinting, crinkling one eye or widening your eyes can send all types of different messages to your fellow speaker.

SKILL BUILDER: Introduce yourself to the class or a small group, trying to look everybody in the eye while you are speaking. After this, attempt conversations with a single person while making eye contact the entire time.

TALKING TIME

Practice this couple's conversation about eating bugs using Talking Tips.

KEVIN	Hey, want to come to my parents' place for dinner tonight? We're eating a traditional Brazilian dish called atta laevigata.
MARILYN	Sure, but what is whatever you said you are eating? What is it?
KEVIN	They are ants.
MARILYN	Ew gross! Why would you eat ants?
KEVIN	Well, they're actually really tasty. They're kind of like salty popcorn.
MARILYN	But who cares? They're bugs.
KEVIN	Bugs are actually really healthy for you. They carry a lot of protein but not a lot of fat.
MARILYN	I'm sorry, I'm not a dietician. What does all of that mean? And why don't you look me in the eyes when you're talking to me. I don't know if you are joking with me or telling the truth.
KEVIN	Oh, I just get nervous speaking with somebody older than me. But the protein in bugs means you get the good nutrition you need, but not the bad stuff you find in beef or pork.
MARILYN	Why not just eat fish? That's healthy for you.
KEVIN	Like I said, this is a traditional dish from my home country, Brazil.
MARILYN	But still, I don't know if I can eat a bug.
KEVIN	Well, you'll never know unless you try!
MARILYN	Okay, you looked me in the eyes this time. I guess I'll give it a shot.

QUESTION TIME

Now answer these questions about the dialog.

1. What does Kevin want to eat with Marilyn?

2. How does Marilyn feel about the meal?

3. What are the good qualities of the meal?

4. Where is Kevin from?

5. Why does Kevin feel nervous about talking with Marylin?

TOPIC STORY

Read this story and talk about the most interesting things in the story.

Waiter, There Aren't Enough Flies in My Soup

Ask most Western people about eating bugs and the most common answer is "Eww, gross." However, entomophagy, or eating insects, is popular all over the world, and becoming a hot new trend for connoisseurs, supermarkets selling the insect dishes and environmentalists.

"The first time I ate witchetty grubs in Australia, they knocked my socks off," said Gavin Conant, a traveling food critic with GoldPoints, a magazine about cuisines from around the world. "These little baby moths tasted just like chicken and almonds, but were so much healthier! I couldn't believe it!"

Witchetty grubs are moth larvae that indigenous people of the Australia Outback eat. These larvae feed on wood, and thus providing many nutrients and most of the necessary protein people need.

In Mexico, a common insect dish is "chapulines (pronounced: cha-poo-lee-nays)," or grasshoppers toasted with lime and garlic. As more Mexican people move to the United States and Canada, grocery stores and food stands are finding it profitable to carry the tangy snack.

"I started selling these grasshopper treats in my shop as a favor to a friend, but also kind of as a joke," said Alex Gills, the owner of Sooper Vee, a specialty food store in Eugene, Oregon. "They killed two birds with one stone. They made a lot of my Mexican customers really happy and made me a lot of money. And I guess they taste good too. I tried them!"

There is also the fact that the raising of insects cuts down on a lot of the pollution that other livestock create. "Insects create less manure, take up less space and do not need to eat as much as cows, pigs, chickens or sheep," said Vitor Straub, co-owner and head scientist of Straub Entomophagists for the Environment, a group that studies and promotes eating bugs. "There are all these benefits to Mother Earth, but also benefits for your health. These edible insects carry all types of vitamins and minerals your daily red meat doesn't have. On top of that, they're almost completely protein and non-fat."

While many people may wrinkle their noses at the idea of eating bugs, some people are rolling the dice and giving them a taste. Whether or not this trend will cross the globe is unknown, but some people are really finding they enjoy them, can earn profits from selling bugs and that eating insects can be good for the earth.

(The Oregonian- Newspaper: February 14, 2014)

COMPREHENSION QUESTIONS

Answer the following questions and write complete sentences.

1. What is entomophagy and why is it becoming popular?

2. How do witchetty grubs taste?

3. Why did Alex Gills start selling chapulines?

4. How can your diet benefit from entomophagy?

5. What are some environmental benefits of raising and eating bugs?

In a group, write and discuss what you think about eating bugs.

What do you think about eating bugs? Should more people give eating bugs a shot? What types of bugs do Koreans eat? What types of odd foods have you tried? Which country has the weirdest food?

HERE'S SOME MORE...

Read about culture from across the globe about today's topic.

Pass the Bundeggi, Please

Some foreigners in Korea are treated to a traditional snack: bundeggi. These are silk worm larva that are steamed or boiled, then seasoned and sold by street vendors or restaurants as a snack for hungry Koreans.

"People eat a lot of gross stuff in this country. I see people going crazy over SPAM. Somebody gave that to me as a Christmas present at my academy and I thought it was a joke," said Katie Plummer, an English teacher at Jump Kids English Academy in Anyang. "SPAM is the grossest stuff I've ever seen. Until somebody offered me bundeggi. Worms? That is beyond gross for me. It's revolting. And when they're being cooked they smell like burning tires. Yuck. Gross."

Westerners generally turn away from dining on insects. It just is not a common thing for them. A television game show called "Fear Factor" featured contestants eating live and cooked bugs, a feat most people found unappetizing.

"I'd rather eat a sewer rat than any of that bug stuff," said Josh Winsett, a commenter on the "Fear Factor" website.

Koreans didn't always eat bundeggi as a snack. Back in the early days when the country was in poverty, many folks didn't have enough money to buy meat or other protein, or simply didn't have access to any. So, they ate bundeggi.

"I actually like it," said Nick Anipen, another English teacher at Jump Kids English Academy. "It's something traditional, and it's not fattening like some other Korean foods. I'm trying to go on a diet so these little guys are just what I need."

(www.BundangForeigners.com- Website: December 2008)

DYNAMITE DISCUSSION

Gather a group and discuss these following questions. When your group finishes, present your ideas to other students.

1. Do you eat bundeggi? What do you think about people who think it is gross?

2. What are other foods from around the world you find weird or unappetizing?

3. How would you react to somebody who said they didn't like Korean people because of some of their traditional foods?

4. If you moved to a foreign country, would you try all of the traditional foods? Why?

5. What do you think about eating bugs instead of meat?

6. Would you go to a restaurant that served only insects? Would you take a date or your parents there? Why?

7. Where do people eat the most insects? Why do you think that is?

8. Which is more important about your food, the environment, health benefits or the taste?

9. How would you collect, raise, feed or cook insects?

10. How has your diet changed since you have aged? What would you like to eat more of when you have more money?

GET IT TOGETHER

Divide into two groups: one group the Pro team and the other the Con team. Write about the pros and cons of eating bugs. Then debate.

1. Do you eat bugs? Why or why not?

____

____

2. Can you convince people that eating bugs is good for their health and the environment?

____

____

3. What are some pros of eating bugs? What are some cons?

Pros:

Cons:

M a s t e r

Lessons for Becoming a Great Conversationalist

D e b a t e

Master

Lessons for Becoming a Great Conversationalist

Debate

Unit 8

Closing Facebook

UNIT 8

ICEBREAKERS

- Do you use Facebook or other social networks? How many times a day? Why?
- What are some weird online activities people get addicted to? Chatting? Posting photos? Computer games?
- Is Facebook good for making and keeping friends? Or a waste of time? Why?

RAPID FIRE

Brainstorm words or sentences related to Facebook.

	Words	Sentences
Noun	Ex) Internet, social network,	
Verb	Ex) To chat,	
Adjective	Ex) Addictive,	

VOCABULARY PREVIEW

Fill in the blank with proper words using the following words.

Refresher	Groundbreaking	Disciplinarian	Cache
Boycott	Conformity	Infuriates	Scrolling down

1. When my friend's daughter comes home late, it __________ her father.
2. The health nuts wanted to __________ all unhealthy food from the school's cafeteria.
3. The prison guard needs to act as a __________ at work.
4. I spend a lot of time on the Internet __________ through different photos.
5. The woman was arrested because the police found a giant __________ of weapons and drugs at her house.

IDIOM TIME! Connect the idioms with their meanings.

Learning idioms will help you sound more like a native speaker, but also, they're fun! Check out these idioms. What do they mean? When would you use them?

1. Under the weather	a. look at
2. FUBAR	b. crowded
3. Packed to the gills	c. crazy
4. One foot off the merry-go-round	d. a bad situation
5. Check out something	e. hungover or sick

Write three sentences with any of the idioms we learned about today.

1. ____

2. ____

3. ____

CONVERSATION

TALKING TIPS

These skills will make you a better English speaker and listener. Pay attention!

Asking Good Questions

Some of the first words you learn in any language are the question words. Many English speakers call them the 5 Ws: who, what, when, where, why and how. We use these words - and others - to find out more information. Here's a refresher on what information you are asking about when using these words:

Who : a person
What : a thing or a fact
When : time, day, year, month, era, etc.
Where : a location or a place
Why : reason
How : method or quality

Now there are other types of questions that don't use these words. We call these "Yes / No Questions." Examples are: "Do you like baseball?" "Can you remember the best meal you ever ate?" "Did I forget to bring a towel?" While sometimes these types of questions can get the answer you want, usually this is just a "Yes" or "No" answer. After these questions, the conversation can die.

However, when asking "5 Ws Questions" or "Good Questions" you can keep the conversation going and flowing. "What is your favorite baseball team?" "Where did you eat your best meal?" "Why should I bring a towel?" So let's try to use Good Questions from now on. We can learn much more about our friends and continue our conversations!

TALKING TIME

Practice this couple's conversation about Facebook using Talking Tips.

COLLEEN Do you like Facebook?

BEN Yes.

COLLEEN That's it? You're going to stop at that?

BEN What do you mean? You just asked if I liked Facebook. You didn't ask me "How often do you check Facebook?" or "Who is your best friend on Facebook?" or "When did you start Facebook?"

COLLEEN Okay, I understand. How about: who was your first friend on Facebook?

BEN My first friend was one of my old university roommates. We called him Matt the Mute, because he was really quiet and never talked. How about you? Who was your first friend on Facebook?

COLLEEN Actually my first friend was my mom. I decided to boycott Facebook but my mom asked me to try it out. Now my Facebook page is packed to the gills with my friends.

BEN Oh cool. Well, what do you do the most with Facebook?

COLLEEN I like chatting with people, but mostly I like to check out other people's photos. It's always interesting to see what other people are doing with their lives.

BEN And sometimes that can be a little weird or spooky.

COLLEEN Yeah. When do you check Facebook?

BEN I check it in the morning when I wake up, and a few times throughout the day.

COLLEEN Wow, asking good questions is a lot better than yes or no questions!

BEN Yup. What would you like to talk about next?

QUESTION TIME

Now answer these questions about the dialog.

1. What is the first question Colleen asks Ben?

2. How does Colleen feel about Ben's first answer? Why?

3. Who was Ben's first friend on Facebook?

4. Who convinced Colleen to start Facebook?

5. How do they use Today's Talking Tip?

TOPIC STORY

Read this story and talk about the most interesting things in the story.

Closing Facebook

South Yatap High School has banned students from using cell phones on school property. While this is not a new rule for most schools on the planet, SYHS created a cellular reception blocker that kills cell phone signals. The blockage covers the entire inside of the building and reaches ten meters outside the school.

"We just noticed our kids were paying too much attention to their social networking sites such as Facebook or Twitter, so we decided to remove the problem from existence," said Bob Erickson, the principal of SYHS. "Right now, there probably isn't a teacher on the planet who hasn't had a class interrupted by a cell phone ringtone. We're stopping that."

The school started construction on this project earlier in the summer and announced this new policy last week. The cell phone-blocking equipment cost the school 5,000,000 won, which came from the school's lunch budget.

"So what if our school lunch isn't any good?" said Erickson. "It wasn't good to begin with. But now we have a grip on these students who try to screw off in class all day. Now they don't get this opportunity to screw off."

As to be expected, students are not enjoying this new rule. "What a stupid jerk! Principal Erickson has one foot off the merry-go-round," said Brad Reilly, a junior at SYHS. "I check Facebook and KakaoTalk with my friends just because class gets so boring! Sometimes I even give notes or today's topic in class or test-taking tips to my friends with my phone. Now I can't even do that! This is such conformity, man!"

While the new development pleases disciplinarians and infuriates students, some teachers feel this step has been too far. "I understand the need to keep kids or students from being distracted, but this is too far. Kids have passed notes since the invention of schools and paper," said John Rictor, a science teacher at SYHS. "But this is ridiculous. What if there is a fire or an emergency at the school and nobody is able to call? That could cause a gigantic problem if you think about it."

Other schools in the area and around the country will monitor the success or failure of this program.

"Why do kids need to check Facebook during class anyway? This is a joke. They are here to learn, not hang out with their friends," said Erickson.

(Yatap Yelp- Newspaper: May 25, 2013)

COMPREHENSION QUESTIONS

Answer the following questions and write complete sentences.

1. What part of the school's budget was cut in order to pay for the cell phone-blocking technology?

2. Find one reason why the South Yatap High School principal wants to ban cell phones.

3. How does Brad Reilly feel about the ban? What did he say about it?

4. What did John Rictor say about the ban?

5. What type of attitude does Principal Erickson seem to have towards children?

In a group, write and discuss what you think about social networking sites.

Write about what you think about the cell phone ban. Should they allow or restrict cell phones at your university? Why or why not? Do you think students would transfer schools if your university blocked cell phones? What type of risks would there be if cell phones were blocked?

HERE'S SOME MORE...

Read about culture from across the globe about today's topic.

Addicted to Facebook

In most tough situations friends can pick you right up, but this young man's friends actually seem to be holding him down.

Travis Golden - who is 29 years old and from San Francisco, California - has not left his house in seven months. He believes if he takes his eyes away from his computer, which constantly shows Facebook, for even a few minutes, he will miss an important update from his giant cache of friends.

"I never know when something cool or funny or interesting will come up," said Golden from his bedroom. "But every time I leave my room I worry that I might miss something. So I try to eat at my computer and sleep with it on. I wake up a few times a night to check updates and photos, or to see if I missed any chats."

Golden lives with his mother who supports her son, but even she wishes he would go out and actually meet the people he knows online. "I don't think he actually knows a single person on that stupid website. He spends half his time scrolling down the News Feed and the other half sending Friend Requests to anybody and everybody. It's ridiculous."

During high school, Golden started on Facebook. However, after graduation he worried he wouldn't talk to friends any more so he started making more friends online. Soon he worried something groundbreaking would happen with his friends and he wouldn't be there to listen, chime in or experience the event.

"I don't know what everybody is fussing about. I don't hurt anybody. Actually, I make friends with people all over the place. All races, religions and countries," said Golden. "Isn't that what we're supposed to do in life? Make friends and be nice to people?"

Mrs. Golden mentioned she is going to call a psychologist if her son doesn't start leaving the house.

(San Francisco Times- Newspaper: February 11, 2013)

DYNAMITE DISCUSSION

Gather a group and discuss these following questions. When your group finishes, present your ideas to other students.

1. Should high schools ban Facebook and cellphones from school property? What about universities? Why or why not?

2. How would you react if your university blocked cell phones on campus?

3. Cellphones can be distracting in class. What are other things that distract students during school?

4. Why do you think people use their phones or mobile devices so much?

5. Which service do you use the most? Facebook? Kakaotalk? Email? Twitter? Instagram? Others?

6. What are some positive things about Facebook or social networking sites? What are some negative things?

7. How often do you check your social network sites or chatting? Why?

8. Some countries made using cell phones while driving illegal. What are some good reasons for this?

9. How has your cell phone use evolved and changed over the years?

10. What are some other weird rules on your campus?

GET IT TOGETHER

Divide into two groups: one group the Pro team and the other the Con team. Write about the pros and cons of Facebook. Then debate.

1. Do you use Facebook? Why or why not? How often?

____

____

2. Should there be limits to people using cell phones, MP3 players, computers or other technologies? How and why?

____

____

3. What are some pros of blocking cell phones or Facebook? What are some cons?

Pros:

Cons:

M a s t e r

Lessons for Becoming a Great Conversationalist

D e b a t e

Master

Lessons for Becoming a Great Conversationalist

Debate

Unit

9

Okay History Is Okay!

UNIT 9

ICEBREAKERS

- What are some weird words or phrases in English? How about in Korean?
- Why do you think English has so many weird words? Why is English such a difficult language to learn?
- How would you change the English language? Vocabulary? Grammar?

RAPID FIRE

Brainstorm words or sentences related to English slang.

	Words	Sentences
Noun	Ex) Slang, different words,	
Verb	Ex) To talk,	
Adjective	Ex) New, different,	

VOCABULARY PREVIEW

Fill in the blank with proper words using the following words.

Assume	Suburb	Slogan	Botched
Mistranslated	Widespread	Derive	Derogatory

1. The ___________ for Frosted Flakes breakfast cereal is "They're GRRRRRRRReat!"
2. The subtitles for the new zombie movie were ___________ so nobody understood the words or plot.
3. During flu season, make sure to wash your hands because the flu virus can be ___________.
4. John ___________ the big play during the last few minutes and lost the baseball game.
5. Many people are fired because they use ___________ remarks and insult their coworkers.

IDIOM TIME! *Connect the idioms with their meanings.*

Learning idioms will help you sound more like a native speaker, but also, they're fun! Check out these idioms. What do they mean? When would you use them?

1. No way	a. I don't believe you
2. In the eyes of...	b. new and easily confused person
3. Chicken scratches	c. you say one thing, I say the other
4. You say 'tomato,' I say 'tomato'	d. someone's opinion
5. Just off the boat	e. poor handwriting

Write three sentences with any of the idioms we learned about today.

1. ____

2. ____

3. ____

CONVERSATION

TALKING TIPS

These skills will make you a better English speaker and listener. Pay attention!

'What's Up?' 'I Don't Care.'

One thing that confuses foreigners when they travel to the United States is the mistranslations of common phrases such as: "What's up?" "How are you doing?" "What's cracking?" "How's it going?" "What's happening?" There are many more similar phrases, but usually the American person isn't actually asking how your day went or how you are feeling. This is just used as a simple greeting. Some Americans might find it weird or funny when people actually answer the question, "What's up?" Generally, most people respond by saying, "What's up?"

A popular beer commercial swept the nation a few years ago. This ad made fun of this common piece of American slang. Men would call each other and say, "Wazzup?" over and over again. Eventually in one of the advertisements somebody actually answered the question and everybody thought he was a boring, crazy person.

So next time somebody says, "How are you doing?" try to just say, "Good. How are you doing?"

TALKING TIME

Practice this couple's conversation about "What's up?" using Talking Tips.

TOMMY Hi Jenny. What's up?

JENNY Not much. I bought a new dog the other day. So she has been keeping me up lately. It's kind of annoying but I guess I needed a new hobby. I am also happy with the weather. But I hope it doesn't get too hot. The hot weather...

TOMMY Hold on, hold on. I don't really care.

JENNY About the weather?

TOMMY No. When somebody says, "What's up?" or "How are you doing?" you can just reply, "How are you doing?" If you answer with a real answer, you look like somebody just off the boat.

JENNY Really? I didn't know that. I am from a small suburb in Wisconsin you know.

TOMMY Yeah, nobody really cares.

JENNY Well, I guess now I know. Is there anything else about me that is wrong?

TOMMY Your handwriting looks like chicken scratches.

QUESTION TIME

Now answer these questions about the dialog.

1. What does Jenny do that is wrong?

2. How does Tommy feel about this mistake?

3. Where is Jenny from?

4. What else does Tommy think is wrong with Jenny?

5. How do they use Today's Talking Tip?

TOPIC STORY

Read this story and talk about the most interesting things in the story.

Okay History Is Okay!

"Okay" or "OK" ranks as one of the most popular English or American words in the world. People who don't speak a word of English possibly know the word okay. While this word is widespread, so are the theories to the origin of the word.

One of the biggest beliefs is that "OK" came from US President Martin Van Buren. Van Buren's nickname was Old Kinderhook, which was shortened to OK. While in the White House, Van Buren signed papers and documents "OK." Since this took less time than signing an entire name, later, "OK" became a way to quickly move something along. During Van Buren's reelection campaign, his campaign managers made "OK" his slogan. Even though the phrase became well-known across the world, Old Kinderhook didn't win his reelection to the White House.

Another related belief comes from a New York social group called The OK Club. If somebody wanted to join the club, the current members would say, "That man is OK."

During the American Civil War in the 1800s, soldiers would write "OK" or "0.K." on a blackboard to signify "Zero Killed." Obviously, this would be a great day in the eyes of the men in the Army.

Misspelling words on purpose became a fad in the 1800s. Therefore, another theory is that "OK" was slang in Boston and New York for "Oll Korrect," meaning "all correct." If this sounds like a silly habit, just remember back when people used purposely misspelled words such as "phat," "bidness" and "kool."

Maybe "okay" isn't even English. Some say the Native American tribal language Chocktaw-Chicksaw could be the base. "Okah" in this language means “it is indeed.” The word could also be derived from a misunderstanding of Scottish Americans saying “och aye!” Other people assume “okay” could come from languages such as French, Mandingo, Finnish, Greek or any number of other languages from around the globe.

Whatever the origin, okay’s history is better than just okay!

(Daily Dictionary- Website: November, 2010)

COMPREHENSION QUESTIONS

Answer the following questions and write complete sentences.

1. What was U.S. President Martin Van Buren's nickname? Why did it become slang?

____

2. How did the United States Army use the phrase OK?

____

3. What did people at the OK Club say about members?

____

4. Why did people purposely misspell words?

____

5. What are some of the other non-English languages that "Okay" could come from?

____

In a group, write and discuss what you think about weird English words.

Write about what you think about English slang. What are some weird examples of English slang? How can you learn or understand all of these words? Should something be done to control slang so the language can be easier to understand? Why do people create so much slang?

____

____

____

____

____

HERE'S SOME MORE...

Read about culture from across the globe about today's topic.

I Speak 'Yankee'

While the New York Yankees are probably one of the most widely known sports teams in the world, or at least in professional baseball, the term "Yankee" has an interesting history. The word has nothing to do with baseball, sports or even the United States. It is actually a mistranslation.

Most people even from the USA do not know where this word originated. Here is one of the possible origin stories: When settlers from England came to the United States they met Native Americans. Eventually, some people of each culture learned the other people's languages.

However, for some reason the Native Americans couldn't easily say the word "English." Instead they botched the word and said, "Yengeese." The English liked the term, but botched it again and said "Yankees." Eventually this term became reserved for English settlers in the New World, and then became the song during the United States Revolution "Yankee Doodle Dandy."

During the US Civil War, Yankee became a word for an American from the Northern States such as Pennsylvania, Massachusetts and New York. Some non-Americans use Yankee as a derogatory insult to Americans. Most Americans just think this is a term of endearment. However, in current times some people from the Southern United States still may be offended by being called "Yankee." In other countries, people still call Americans "Yankees."

(www.DailyDictionary.com- Website: June 2011)

DYNAMITE DISCUSSION

Gather a group and discuss these following questions. When your group finishes, present your ideas to other students.

1. What are interesting slang words or terms in English?

2. Why do you think there is so much slang in English?

3. How can people better understand all of this slang?

4. What are some types of slang differences in Korean?

5. If you don't understand a slang word, where do you look for the meaning?

6. "Yankee" is a term for people from the USA. What are other terms for people from other countries?

7. Why are some people offended by these terms?

8. Have you ever created slang with your friends? What was it?

9. What are some other popular words from English that are now used in everyday Korean?

10. What are some Korean words that should be used all over the world?

GET IT TOGETHER

Divide into two groups: one group the Pro team and the other the Con team. Write about the pros and cons of slang. Then debate.

1. When you speak English, do you use slang? Why or why not?

____

____

2. Who uses slang? What type of people use slang? When is slang proper or improper to use? Where does slang come from?

____

____

3. What are some pros of slang? What are some cons?

Pros:

Cons:

Master

Lessons for Becoming a Great Conversationalist

Debate

Master

Lessons for Becoming a Great Conversationalist

Debate

Unit 10

The Right Age Go Look Good

UNIT 10

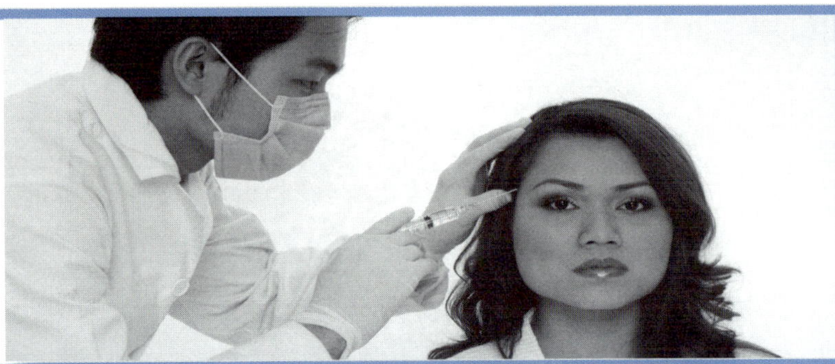

ICEBREAKERS

- Why do you think so many people receive plastic surgery?
- Which plastic surgeries are popular in Korea? How about the Western World? Why?
- If you could get plastic surgery, what would you get?

RAPID FIRE

Brainstorm words or sentences related to plastic surgery.

	Words	Sentences
Noun	Ex) Plastic surgery, appearance,	
Verb	Ex) To improve,	
Adjective	Ex) Attractive,	

VOCABULARY PREVIEW

Fill in the blank with proper words using the following words.

Liposuction	Cut-rate	Procedure	Preposterous
Recipients	Amputate	Vain	Peers

1. The model was so __________ when she talked because she was always looking in her mirror.
2. My doctor did the medical __________ to fix my back and it didn't even hurt that much!
3. When I sent my car to the __________ mechanic, at first I saved a lot of money but then my car broke down again very quickly.
4. The politicians discuss with their fellow __________ to learn what their vote on the new law should be.
5. Since he gained so much weight, he wanted to get __________ to appear skinny again.

IDIOM TIME! *Connect the idioms with their meanings.*

Learning idioms will help you sound more like a native speaker, but also, they're fun! Check out these idioms. What do they mean? When would you use them?

1. Plain Jane	a. respect something
2. Getting work done	b. a perfect example
3. Over my head	c. a person who isn't particularly attractive
4. Posterchild	d. hard to understand
5. Hold high	e. receiving plastic surgery

Write three sentences with any of the idioms we learned about today.

1. ______________________________

2. ______________________________

3. ______________________________

CONVERSATION

TALKING TIPS

These skills will make you a better English speaker and listener. Pay attention!

Disagreeing With Someone

Arguing with anybody can be difficult. Instead of simply saying, "You are wrong," there are other more proper ways to disagree with somebody.

If your partner wants to do something you do not agree with, say, "Why would you want to do that?" If they want to make a big change in their life, appearance or job, you can say, "I think _______ is fine the way it is."

Another thing to do is explain why you think somebody is wrong. You can say, "The reason I don't agree with you is _______." Or you could try, "I disagree with you. Here is why...".

While giving reasons why the person is wrong, it is also a great idea to ask logical questions concerning your disagreement. Does the person want to grow a beard? Ask them if they like to scratch their face all the time. Ask if they like looking dirty. Ask if their romantic partner will like it.

TALKING TIME

Practice this couple's conversation about plastic surgery using Talking Tips.

TED	I'm thinking about getting a nosejob.
VICTORIA	Why would you want to do that? Your nose looks fine to me.
TED	Yeah, but I feel like it's too big. I always felt weird about it. Everybody in my family has perfect-looking noses, and I just feel left out.

VICTORIA Maybe instead of feeling left out, you could feel unique! You're different, and that always isn't a bad thing.

TED That's a good point. However, this may sound weird, but one of my ex-girlfriends got breast implants and her self-confidence went through the roof afterwards! I want that to happen to me.

VICTORIA But what if this operation isn't enough to bring up your confidence? Or worse yet, what if something goes horribly wrong?

TED That would be awful, but this is just a nosejob. Doctors do these every day and nobody gets hurt.

VICTORIA Okay, well, what about all the money you spend on this? Couldn't you use it another way to make yourself feel better?

TED Yeah, but you buy new clothes to make ourselves feel better. People exercise to make themselves feel better. What's wrong with me wanting to change something on my face to make me feel better?

VICTORIA I wish you the best of luck, but I still think you look fine to me.

QUESTION TIME

Now answer these questions about the dialog.

1. What does Ted want?

2. How does Victoria try to talk him out of it?

3. How does Ted feel different than his family?

4. What do you think is Ted's best reason for doing what he wants to do?

5. How do they use Today's Talking Tip?

TOPIC STORY

Read this story and talk about the most interesting things in the story.

The Right Age to Look Good

If you want to get that nosejob, breast implants or liposuction, you might need to show some ID soon. Confidence for Korean Kids - a new parents' group in Korea - is attempting to make a law to require plastic surgery recipients to show proof they are at least 19 years of age before consulting with a doctor.

"Why do we allow children to receive unnecessary surgeries before they are even allowed to drink alcohol or smoke cigarettes? While drinking and smoking aren't safe either, at least the effects aren't usually permanent," said Doug Reimer, the president and spokesman of Confidence for Korean Kids.

In the past few years, Korea has become a hot spot for plastic surgery. All throughout Korea, there are many different clinics with many different varieties of surgeries, as well as skill levels of the surgeons.

"Our youngsters are getting unnecessary plastic surgeries at younger and younger ages. Whether it's cutting the double eyelid or strengthening the chin, these surgeries cost a lot of money," said Reimer. "Not all families have the money for the most expensive doctors, so they visit cut-rate clinics and end up butchered."

Even though plastic surgery grows safer every year, there are still accidents. Josephina Cooper, an American, hoped an operation breaking her legs to insert titanium rods would make her taller. The procedure worked, but only for a while. A week after the surgery, Cooper's body rejected the implants causing an infection and complications that forced emergency doctors to amputate both of Cooper's legs.

"I never thought it could happen to me, but it did. Just because I was vain and wanted to be a little bit taller, I ended up losing both my legs," said Cooper, in a prepared statement. Since her accident, Cooper has become the posterchild for Confidence for Korean Kids movement. "If I could have just been happy with myself I would never have had so many of these problems."

As to be expected, many plastic surgeons and clinic owners are not happy about the possible age requirement for operations. "I find this preposterous and ridiculous that an entire profession is being punished for just a few idiots who shouldn't practice medicine anyway," said Dr. Jenna Reed, from Apgujung Beauty Works, a plastic surgery clinic. "I've been operating on children and adults for 17 years and never once had a malpractice suit filed against me. If people have the money and the desire for a procedure, why should we stop them? Why should a Plain Jane live her life as a Plain Jane?"

Confidence for Korean Kids holds information sessions about the dangers and costs of plastic surgery for concerned parents and children. In the past they protested outside of doctors' offices, appeared on numerous television programs and even pass out anti-surgery flyers in areas with high concentrations of plastic surgery clinics. The new age requirement for plastic surgery law will be voted on during the next election this March.

"Being better looking or taller won't instantly raise your self-esteem. Most of us don't learn that until we are older, but if we can pass that knowledge onto our children before they make these permanent mistakes, we can save them a lot of trouble and in the long run have more confident children. Who wouldn't want that?"

To counter this viewpoint, plastic surgeons say they provide a much-needed service for people. "We all want our children and friends to feel better about themselves," said Dr. Reed. "While much beauty can be found within, sometimes plastic surgery can give a person the push to become a more confident individual."

(www.AtlasofApgu.gov- Website: January, 2013)

COMPREHENSION QUESTIONS

Answer the following questions and write complete sentences.

1. Why does Confidence for Korean Kids want to change the laws on plastic surgery?

2. According to Doug Reimer, where do poor families go to receive plastic surgery they can afford?

3. How has Confidence for Korean Kids tried to spread the word about the dangers of plastic surgery?

4. Where is the Beauty Works clinic located?

5. What are plastic surgeons saying to defend their profession and actions?

In a group, write and discuss what you think about plastic surgery.

Write about what you think about plastic surgery. What are some popular plastic surgery procedures? Why do so many Koreans see plastic surgeons? How can people feel better about themselves? Would you ever get plastic surgery? What?

HERE'S SOME MORE...

Read about culture from across the globe about today's topic.

A Deeper Voice for Deeper Pockets

A few years ago a new study from New York University's psychology department found that men and women with deeper voices were more respected by their peers, and therefore made more money and appeared more attractive to potential boyfriends and girlfriends.

Now, a plastic surgeon is offering an operation that could lower your voice, but the price may be more than what people bargained for. "When I heard people with baritone (lower) voices earned higher salaries, I thought this would be a great opportunity to start a new surgery to equal the playing field for everyone," said Dr. Kenny Scolari, the head plastic surgeon of Milwaukee Cup of Life Clinic. "Now anybody can speak in a deep, sultry voice that people respect and hold up high."

The operation is too complicated to go into detail in this article, but mainly requires the vocal cords to be severed, then retied and tightened. All patients lose their voices for about a week, and a small percentage never recover their speaking abilities. A tinier fraction of people lose the ability to sing or speak quickly, but in most cases the person ends up with a deeper voice.

Opponents of the surgery say not enough studies have been done. "We have absolutely no idea what the long-term effects of this surgery could be," said Matt Parker, a health advocate for the Denslow Group, a public protection agency. "We have people losing their voices permanently. And for what? A study that says you can make more money? Is that really worth being mute for the rest of your life?"

(New York Post- Newspaper: May 29, 2003)

DYNAMITE DISCUSSION

Gather a group and discuss these following questions. When your group finishes, present your ideas to other students.

1. What are some popular plastic surgeries in Korea? In the Western world?

2. Why do you think so many people go for plastic surgery?

3. What are some dangers of plastic surgery?

4. Where on their bodies do people get the most plastic surgery? Face? Eyes? Hands? Breasts?

5. Would you get plastic surgery? Where? Why?

6. When should people be allowed to receive plastic surgery?

7. What types of advice or kind words could you say to cheer up an unattractive friend?

8. How do people or their confidence levels change after plastic surgery?

9. How do you feel about people with a lot of work done?

10. If two ugly people receive plastic surgery and then marry, what types of children will they have?

GET IT TOGETHER

Divide into two groups: one group the Pro team and the other the Con team. Write about the pros and cons of plastic surgery. Then debate.

1. Some people disagree with plastic surgery and think that the money could be used for life-saving surgeries. What do you think?

____

____

2. Who gets plastic surgery? Why? What are some common accidents with plastic surgery? Where do people in Korea go for it? When are people ready for it?

____

____

3. What are some pros of plastic surgery? What are some cons?

Pros:

Cons:

M a s t e r

Lessons for Becoming a Great Conversationalist

D e b a t e

Master

Lessons for Becoming a Great Conversationalist

Debate

Unit

11

Love Is in the Air, Grab Your Wallet

UNIT 11

ICEBREAKERS

▷▷Are many of your friends getting married? How does that make you feel?

▷▷At what age would you like to get married?

▷▷How much do you want to spend on your wedding? What will you spend your money on?

RAPID FIRE

Brainstorm words or sentences related to weddings.

	Words	Sentences
Noun	Ex) Weddings, budget,	______________________________ ______________________________
Verb	Ex) To spend,	______________________________ ______________________________
Adjective	Ex) Happy,	______________________________ ______________________________

VOCABULARY PREVIEW

Fill in the blank with proper words using the following words.

Metalheads	Cheapskates	Intimacy	Chapel
Odds and ends	Bestow	Legendary	Drive-through

1. Those __________ didn't leave their waitress enough money!
2. I don't like to go inside of restaurants, so I go to the __________ of most fast food places.
3. If you go to a hard rock concert, you might see a lot of __________.
4. When I move to a new home I pack different __________ that I keep around my house.
5. The girl's dad wanted to __________ the company to his daughter after he died.

IDIOM TIME! *Connect the idioms with their meanings.*

Learning idioms will help you sound more like a native speaker, but also, they're fun! Check out these idioms. What do they mean? When would you use them?

1. Tie the knot	a. the couple's celebration after a wedding
2. Honeymoon	b. reserve something – usually money – for another time
3. Tighten your belt	c. close to winning, but never winning
4. Save for a rainy day	d. to get married
5. Always a bridesmaid, never a bride	e. cut down on spending or extra things

Write three sentences with any of the idioms we learned about today.

1. ______________________________
2. ______________________________
3. ______________________________

CONVERSATION

TALKING TIPS

These skills will make you a better English speaker and listener. Pay attention!

Bring Smiles To Other Faces

Everybody gets frustrated sometimes. Cheering somebody up in any language can be difficult, but it's something important to do in many different situations. Sometimes you can find a famous quote from another person to make somebody a bit happier. You can start this quote by saying, "This person says this quote." Here are some examples:

"I know you are unhappy right now, but Arnold Glasgow says, *Nothing lasts forever. Not even your troubles*."

"Oscar Wilde said, *Life is far too important to be taken seriously*. I hope that makes your day better."

"When I am sad, my mom always says, *Don't frown. You never know when somebody is falling in love with your smile*."

So next time somebody needs some cheering up, give them some good advice from somebody else!

TALKING TIME

Practice this couple's conversation about weddings using Talking Tips.

BRIAN Planning for our wedding is so stressful. We need to rent a wedding hall, pick out invitations, send out invitations, buy presents, and then find the right cakes, tuxes and dresses! I feel like I'm going to go crazy!

YVONNE Whenever I get stressed out around my dad he says, "*Happiness is hard work. Get at it*."

BRIAN: But I am so tired! There's so much work and the wedding is less than a month away.

YVONNE: Yes, but once we're finished we'll be so happy to have the perfect wedding.

BRIAN: Do you really think there is such a thing as a perfect wedding?

YVONNE: Of course I do. If we are in love, our friends and family are happy and we snap enough photos I think our wedding will be perfect.

BRIAN: There are so many things that can go wrong. What if it rains? What if people don't like the food? What if our families don't like each other?

YVONNE: My friend Duke always says, "*There are a lot of what ifs. You're too smart for that*." At the end of our big day, as long as we are in love and say "I do" I don't think anything bad can happen. All the flowers, big cakes and dresses in the world won't save a couple that isn't in love.

BRIAN: I guess if you put it that way. Now comes a really stressful part. What kind of music do you want at the wedding dance? I would like rock & roll, hard rock, classic rock, punk rock and heavy metal. How about you?

YVONNE: That kind of music is a sure bet to have an awful wedding. My sister Daisy says, "*There's a reason so many heavy metalheads are single*."

QUESTION TIME

Now answer these questions about the dialog.

1. Why is Brian so stressed out?

2. How does Yvonne's dad feel about happiness?

3. When are they getting married?

4. What type of music does Brian want at his wedding?

5. Who are all the people Yvonne quoted?

TOPIC STORY

Read this story and talk about the most interesting things in the story.

Love Is in the Air, Grab Your Wallet

What would you do with 100,000,000 won? Would you buy a new car? Would you take the vacation of a lifetime? Pay off your student debt? Put the money in the bank for your children's education? Save it for a rainy day? Or just get married? The Hankuk Cultural Studies Group (HCSG) discovered that the average Korean Wedding now costs nearly four times as much as the average American wedding. Over the years the price of a Korean wedding shot up to 100,000,000 won, while the price of an average American wedding sits at about 25,000,000 won. With those numbers, you could get married four times in the States for the price of just one Korean wedding!

"Most people think that Americans are the world's biggest wedding spenders, but that simply isn't true anymore," says Myung-Ku Lim of the HCSG. "We're seeing Koreans spending much more. The reasons are Korean men put a huge down payment on a house, buy so many gifts for guests, rent the wedding hall or church, stock the buffet and find so many other odds and ends that add up to a hefty sum."

There are many differences between a Korean and American wedding. The first is the invitation list. Americans generally invite about 100 to 200 people, and usually those people are close family, friends and neighbors. However, Koreans invite family, friends, coworkers, neighbors as well as the parents' coworkers and neighbors.

Koreans expect guests to give a gift of money to help pay for wedding costs and help the newlyweds start their new life together. "Usually this cash is a great help, but there are always a few cheapskates in the crowd. Feeding large groups is expensive in any country, but some guests show up to the buffet and don't bestow a gift to the married couple," says Lim.

Korean wedding halls are a common sight for anybody traveling down a Korean street. However, some young Koreans are fed up with the lack of intimacy, the rush and the cost of wedding halls. A rising trend in Korea seems to be getting married in a courthouse, holding smaller ceremonies or a destination wedding. A destination wedding is when a couple travels to another country to be married. Popular weddings spots are Thailand, Mexico and even the United States.

"My husband and I had our wedding in Hawaii and it was a totally different and beautiful experience," says Diana Ahn, of Suwon. "While everybody we knew couldn't come to the service, the people who did come were our close friends and remained quiet during our wedding." Since American weddings are in churches, it is considered bad manners to speak, check your phone or stand up during the wedding procession.

"I also liked having bridesmaids and my husband loved having groomsmen. They made the experience much friendlier," says Ahn. Bridesmaids are usually the bride's best female friends or sisters and usually help the bride with her makeup, hair and dress. The number one bridesmaid is called the maid of honor. The groomsmen are the groom's best male friends or brothers. The number one groomsman is called the best man.

During dinner in an American wedding, the best man and maid of honor usually give speeches about the groom and bride. They can recount stories about growing up, talk about how the couple met and even give advice to the newlyweds.

An American wedding isn't over when the food is finished. Ahn explains, "After the meal we had the best part of an American wedding: the wedding dance!" A wedding dance usually follows the nuptials in an American wedding. This is usually held in a hotel auditorium, a bar or any type of convention center. This is a chance for the guests and bridal couple to celebrate, dance, drink and eat cake. The music is supplied by a band or a deejay. This can be when the bride throws the bouquet into a crowd of unmarried women, everybody does the Chicken Dance or any number of different traditions.

While the entirety of a Korean wedding may last only an hour or two, an

American wedding service lasts about an hour. After that, there is eating, speeches and the wedding dance, which usually take up most of a day or night.

"I doubt we will see Koreans change too many of their wedding habits, because we have so much tradition in this country. On the other side, I think it is important for young people to know they have other options instead of digging themselves into a gigantic debt," says Kim.

In the end, it is up to the couple how and where they want to wed. If they want to tie the knot in Korea, they better tighten their belts for a while!

(Korean Nuptial News- Weekly Newspaper: August 15, 2013)

COMPREHENSION QUESTIONS

Answer the following questions and write complete sentences.

1. What are three differences between a Korean and American weddings.

____

2. What is a "destination wedding?"

____

3. Write three differences between Korean and American weddings.

____

4. What happens at an American wedding dance?

____

5. Why does Myung-Ku Kim of the HCGS think that Koreans wedding trends will continue?

____

In a group, write and discuss what you think about weddings.

Free write about whatever you can think of on the topic of weddings. Do you think people get married too young or too old? How much do you spend to plan on your wedding? Where will you have it? What do you like about Korean traditions or American traditions?

____

____

____

____

____

HERE'S SOME MORE...

Read about culture from across the globe about today's topic.

The City of Sin...And Love?

Where do more people get married than any other city in the world? Is it romantic Paris? Historic Rome? The beautiful beaches of Hawaii? Nope. It's Las Vegas!

They call Las Vegas "The City of Sin" because of the casinos, legendary parties, clubs and all types of other fun, but another thing Vegas is famous for is weddings! Why? Well, early in the city's formation, they made it very fast, cheap and easy for couples to get married. And it's still fast, cheap and easy to be wed in Vegas.

As you drive through Las Vegas you can see famous wedding chapels. You can show up, fill out some paperwork, pay a fee of anywhere from $50 to $200, exchange vows and be on your way! There are even themed-wedding chapels. You can have an Elvis Presley impersonator as your minister! You can get married wearing your bikini or swim trunks! There's even a drive-through wedding service! You won't even need to leave your car!

While some say Vegas weddings lack romance, class or tradition, some say the quick pace, cheap cost and low hassle make the experience perfect for couples on-the-go, on a budget and looking for a stress-free way to get married.

(www.FunStuff.com- Website: August 2008)

DYNAMITE DISCUSSION

Gather a group and discuss these following questions. When your group finishes, present your ideas to other students.

1. Are weddings too expensive? What are the biggest costs? How could you make them cheaper?

2. Where do you want to get married? When? To whom?

3. Who will you invite to your wedding? Friends, family, coworkers, neighbors, your parents' coworkers and neighbors?

4. What gifts do you give at weddings?

5. What are some rude things to do at a wedding?

6. Talk about your opinions on marrying in Las Vegas. Would you do it? Why or why not?

7. What are some strange wedding traditions in Korea? From around the world?

8. How do you celebrate after a wedding?

9. Where would you go for your honeymoon?

10. Why do so many people get divorced?

GET IT TOGETHER

Divide into two groups: one group the Pro team and the other the Con team. Write about the pros and cons of weddings. Then debate.

1. What do you think about marriage? Is it a touchy subject? Why?

2. What makes weddings so pricey? Would you want a cheap wedding and have more money for the future, or experience a really nice wedding and start your new life out in deep debt?

3. Would you get married in Las Vegas? Why or why not? Write some pros and cons!

Pros:

Cons:

Unit 12

Making English Easier

UNIT 12

ICEBREAKERS

▷▷What is the hardest part about learning English? Reading, writing, listening or speaking?

▷▷What would you like to change about English?

▷▷People say we are always getting dumber. What do you think?

RAPID FIRE

Brainstorm words or sentences related to English.

	Words	Sentences
Noun	Ex) English, changes,	
Verb	Ex) To learn,	
Adjective	Ex) Easy,	

VOCABULARY PREVIEW

Fill in the blank with proper words using the following words.

Everlasting	Grueling	Bothersome	Redundancy
Accessible	Snafus	Confound	Vetoed

1. That long and boring movie felt like it was ___________.
2. Picking up all the trash after a big festival can be very ___________.
3. In order to save time, our company is trying to cut down on ___________ and wasteful spending.
4. The politicians ___________ the new rule that would allow recreational drug use.
5. Make sure that the stairs are ___________ to handicapped people.

IDIOM TIME! *Connect the idioms with their meanings.*

Learning idioms will help you sound more like a native speaker, but also, they're fun! Check out these idioms. What do they mean? When would you use them?

1. Jumping for joy	a. make something simpler
2. Around the globe	b. something popular all over
3. Shortlisted	c. to be very excited
4. Dumbing down	d. somebody or something that is a top choice
5. Get rid of	e. dispose of something

Write three sentences with any of the idioms we learned about today.

1. ____
2. ____
3. ____

CONVERSATION

TALKING TIPS

These skills will make you a better English speaker and listener. Pay attention!

Words From All Over

English has so many words from all over the planet! But try not to get too frustrated trying to learn them. Nobody knows all the words and English dictionaries change all the time. If you don't understand a word, just ask somebody, "I'm sorry, can you repeat that last word?" or "I don't know the meaning of that word."

Don't worry about sounding dumb. People know English is your second language and even native speakers ask questions about words they don't understand. Remember, asking questions helps us learn better, faster and more.

TALKING TIME

Practice this couple's conversation about English using Talking Tips.

CHRIS I am not having one of my best days.

LEAH Why are you so unhappy?

CHRIS I hate learning English!

LEAH Why is that, Chris?

CHRIS There are so many words. I don't understand these words "time consuming."

LEAH "Time consuming" means something that takes up a lot of time. Once you learn all of English's grammar, spellings and words, isn't it a great language?

CHRIS What are you talking about?

LEAH Think about all the great literature written in English. There is Shakespeare, Ernest Hemingway and James Joyce. Or even new books like "Harry Potter" or "Twilight!" It's magnificent!

CHRIS See, I don't know what "magnificent" means either.

LEAH That means wonderful. But think of all the history behind the English language.

CHRIS Who cares? Everybody used to speak Latin, now nobody does. English is a waste of time.

LEAH I think you need to consider how many people in the world speak English now. I think this language is everlasting. Do you know that word?

CHRIS Oh, I know that. It means something that lasts forever. I suppose I'll have to study English no matter what. I wish it would change.

LEAH You never know! Maybe you'll get a girlfriend to help you learn English! That would be super duper!

CHRIS I don't even want to know what that stupid word means.

QUESTION TIME

Now answer these questions about the dialog.

1. What is Chris' problem?

2. How does Leah feel about English?

3. Which book authors does Leah like?

4. Which word of Leah's does Chris understand?

5. What do you think "super duper" means?

TOPIC STORY

Read this story and talk about the most interesting things in the story.

Making English Easier

As you probably know, learning, speaking, listening, reading, writing and understanding in the English language is difficult. Some say English is one of the most difficult languages to learn, let alone master. There are an incredible amount of weird words, a wide variety of accents, grueling grammar guidelines, impossible-to-follow rules, difficult-to-remember irregularities, spelling snafus and bothersome pronunciation.

Well, one group is hoping to help you and everybody else who is having a tough time learning English. The REAL Group (REAL stands for "Reforming English for All Learners") hopes to change some of the more difficult grammar rules and spellings to make English an easier-to-learn language.

"We've decided enough is enough. No language should be this hard to learn," said Daphne Nelson, the president of the REAL Group and a high school English teacher at Tehachapi High School in Tehachapi, California. "As a teacher, I am constantly asked questions such as, 'Why is phone spelled with a ph?' I am tired of answering, 'Well, because 2,000 years ago some Romans spoke Latin and they made an eff sound with a ph. And for some reason, English decided to take on a lot of Latin's spellings and rules.'"

Nelson believes that changing English will make the language easier and more accessible. "If English is going to be the global language, it needs to adapt to today's society," she said. "People don't have time or patience to learn all the idiosyncrasies of the English language." The REAL Group stated in a press release:

"The English language has already gone through three major changes. What is now known as Old English was spoken about the time 'Beowulf' was written.

Middle English was spoken around the time 'Canterbury Tales' was written. Modern English hasn't changed that much since William Shakespeare wrote his plays. All these big changes came because English speakers wanted to include more people into the language. Now that much of the world is speaking English, we need to facilitate people's understanding of the English language. To do this, we believe it's time to create new rules, spellings and grammar for the English language. We can call it Postmodern English or New English or Neo English. It's time for a change!"

This new way to read and write English could make students around the globe happier, but not everybody is jumping for joy. Nick Bork, an English professor in Nebraska said, "These rules have been in our language for hundreds of years. Why should we change now? Why did I spend all my time learning and teaching English just to purge it all away? We are proud to speak the way we speak. We don't need to dumb this language down any more."

Some of the proposed changes would be like spelling without the Silent C. With the new rule "Duck" would be spelled as "Duk." Also shortlisted for spelling changes would be knight, school and friend. With the new spellings these words would look like "nite, skool and frend."

REAL Group would also get rid of changing pronouns. Instead of I, me, my and myself, all first-person pronouns would change into me. So instead of saying, "I baked all my bread by myself and served it to my family and me," you would say, "Me baked all me bread by me and served it to me family and me."

Nelson explained, "These new spellings and grammar rules may confound some old speakers and confuse a generation or two, but the fact of the matter is, we need to change and we need to change now. Our descendants will thank us. Also, the REAL Group plans to reduce the redundancy of words, like confound and confuse. Why do we need two words that mean exactly the same thing? The fact is, we don't."

(Tehachapi Times- Newspaper: April 10, 2013)

COMPREHENSION QUESTIONS

Answer the following questions and write complete sentences.

1. What does the REAL Group want?

____

2. What is the argument to keep English the same?

____

3. Why does Daphne Nelson want to get rid of either confound or confuse?

____

4. With the new rules, how do you think we would write this sentence, "I gave my best friend my favorite picture of myself?"

____

5. With the new rules, how do you think we would spell words like Fight, Learn, Guide and Health?

____

In a group, write and discuss what you think about English.

Free write about whatever you can think of on the topic of the English language. Do you think it is a good language? Why or why not? What do you think about the proposed changes to the language? What would you do to make English easier?

____

____

____

____

____

HERE'S SOME MORE...

Read about culture from across the globe about today's topic.

A New, Easy-to-Use Language!

Kiel Vi Fartas?

If you have no idea what the above sentence - "Kiel Vi Fartas?" - means, don't worry, you're not alone. This sentence is Esperanto for "How are you?" What is Esperanto? Well, here you go!

In 1887 L. L. Zamenhof created the language Esperanto and hoped that it would be an easy-to-learn language that would break down political and language barriers between people. Esperanto quickly gained popularity with world leaders because if everybody spoke the same language, everybody could speak! At one time, the League of Nations (the precursor to the United Nations) voted to make Esperanto the League's official language. However, the French delegate vetoed the proposal because he worried that French would no longer be an international language.

Esperanto started growing bigger and bigger, but World War II changed most of that. Adolph Hitler of Nazi Germany persecuted Zamenhof and his language, mostly because Zamenhof was Jewish. Josef Stalin of the USSR and the emperor of Japan both made speaking Esperanto illegal in their countries. Stalin believed the Esperanto was "the language of spies" and the Japanese emperor claimed Esperanto speakers were "too peace-loving."

Estimates claim there are anywhere from 10,000 to 2 million active or fluent speakers of this interesting language. Esperanto speakers live all over the world, but most populations live in Europe, East Asia or South America.

There are 28 letters in the language and word order is mostly free, which means you can put nouns, verbs, adjectives, prepositions or anything else you can think of wherever you like! The vocabulary is so easy, you can even make up new words as you are speaking and your friends will probably understand you!

(www.DailyDictionary.com- Website: April 2005)

DYNAMITE DISCUSSION

Gather a group and discuss these following questions. When your group finishes, present your ideas to other students.

1. Is learning Esperanto useful? Why or why not?

2. Would you learn Esperanto? Why or why not?

3. When do you think English became a global language?

4. Where is English spoken? Why?

5. What do you think about REAL's changes to English? Are they good ideas?

6. How can English become an easier-to-learn language? Give examples.

7. How can you communicate with somebody who doesn't speak your language?

8. Braille, sign language and writing are all other types of communication. Can you think of any others?

9. How can you get more people to speak Korean?

10. Besides Korea, where do the most people speak Korean?

GET IT TOGETHER

Divide into two groups: one group the Pro team and the other the Con team. Write about the pros and cons of English and other global languages. Then debate.

1. What are some reasons to have a global language? What do you lose if you don't speak your language? Imagine that instead of saying "kimchi" you just said, "red spicy cabbage." How would that make you feel?

____

____

2. What makes English so difficult to learn or translate? How would you change things?

____

____

3. What are some pros and cons of making Korean a global language?

Pros:

Cons:

Master

Lessons for Becoming a Great Conversationalist

Debate

Master

Lessons for Becoming a Great Conversationalist

Debate

Unit 13

Not in Our Name

UNIT 13

ICEBREAKERS

- What would you name your own sports team?
- What are some of your favorite team, theme park or advertising mascots?
- When you think of Native Americans, Aboriginals or Indigenous People, what do you think about?

RAPID FIRE

Brainstorm words or sentences related to sports mascots.

	Words	Sentences
Noun	Ex) Sports, mascots,	
Verb	Ex) To cheer,	
Adjective	Ex) Offensive,	

VOCABULARY PREVIEW

Fill in the blank with proper words using the following words.

Mascot	Controversial	Likenesses	Masculinity
Leprechaun	Ridiculed	Ferocity	Portrayals

1. At the zoo, the tiger showed her __________ by growling and then attacking her cage.
2. Drugs and birth control are a very __________ topic to discuss with just about anybody.
3. The weight lifter displays his __________ by showing off his big muscles.
4. My favorite __________ for a company is Mickey Mouse.
5. All the performers in the play were awarded special trophies for their __________ of the king, queen and royal court members.

IDIOM TIME! *Connect the idioms with their meanings.*

Learning idioms will help you sound more like a native speaker, but also, they're fun! Check out these idioms. What do they mean? When would you use them?

1. Like mad	a. not seriously intended
2. Make a big deal	b. to act crazy
3. Whitey	c. show how important something is
4. Tongue in cheek	d. act stronger
5. Man up	e. a derogatory term for a white person

Write three sentences with any of the idioms we learned about today.

1. ______________________________

2. ______________________________

3. ______________________________

CONVERSATION

TALKING TIPS

These skills will make you a better English speaker and listener. Pay attention!

What's Your Opinion?

Everybody is entitled to an opinion, and they can be very different depending on the person. Discussing opinions is a very common thing to do with friends, family and even strangers.

Some people love to blab about their opinions, while others don't like to give up their opinions so easily. If you want to ask somebody's opinion, you can say, "What are your thoughts about _______?" or "How do you feel about _______?"

If you want to answer somebody's question about your opinion, you can start with, "I feel / think / believe that _______." Make sure to give good reasons why you feel / think / believe the way you do!

TALKING TIME

Practice this couple's conversation about mascots using Talking Tips.

ROB Check out my new Washington Redskins hat! What do you think? It's totally awesome, isn't it?

ANDY No way! In my opinion, and many other people's opinions, that's a totally offensive hat. Look at that Native American mascot! He looks like an animal!

ROB Oh come on, who cares?

ANDY Think about it. How would you feel if your race, religion or nationality was made into a cartoon mascot?

ROB Eh, I beg to differ with you. First, who do Americans respect more than their athletes or sports teams?

ANDY How about the name The Redskins. Boy oh boy, it doesn't get much more racist than that! How would you feel if they were the Colored Boys? The White Trash Guys? The Dirty Spics, Micks or Hicks?

ROB I've been a Redskins fan my entire life. I love them! I feel like we're doing a favor to Native Americans. I think if we didn't put them as our sports mascots, they'd probably be forgotten by now.

ANDY So you want an entire group of people to be remembered as naked warriors with bows and arrows that represent a football team?

ROB Look at the Notre Dame Fightin' Irish. Their mascot is a leprechaun Irishman who jumps around like mad. You don't see Irish people getting mad about that. Or the Minnesota Vikings? The Vikings were an actual group of people. Why don't people protest that name?

ANDY Maybe because the Vikings and Irish people are represented in other ways besides wild sports mascots.

ROB The name is just a name. I don't see what you're making a big deal about.

ANDY Exactly, if the name is just a name, why don't they change the mascot to the Washingon Wildcats or something that isn't offensive or racist?

QUESTION TIME

Now answer these questions about the dialog.

1. How does Andy feel about Rob's hat?
2. How does Rob defend his team's mascot?
3. What are two other teams Rob mentions with mascots that are actually groups of people?
4. How do they use today's Talking Tips?
5. What does Andy want the team to change their name to?

TOPIC STORY

Read this story and talk about the most interesting things in the story.

Not in Our Name

The Cleveland Indians, the Kansas City Chiefs and Washington Redskins are some of the most popular sports teams in the United States. These teams also use some of the most controversial mascots. Native American people do not like that their tribal names and likenesses are used and often ridiculed during sporting events. On the other hand, sports fans say the mascot names are tributes to the Native American people and their bravery, ferocity or masculinity.

Native mascots are often depicted as big-nosed, nearly naked warriors who wear feather headdresses and carry bows, arrows, tomahawks or spears. Native Americans, also called Natives, indigenous people or American Indians, find many faults with these derogatory portrayals and say the mascots are racist, hostile, abusive and insensitive.

"This is a human rights issue. We are being denied the most basic respect. As long as our people are perceived as cartoon characters, our socio-economic problems will never be seriously addressed," said Michael S. Haney, a Native America rights activist.

Before games, sometimes a rival team's fans will attempt to offend a Native-named team by making signs that say, "Scalp 'em!" or "Indians Suck!" Also, pictures of Native people being beaten, killed or embarrassed are distributed around stadium areas. On top of that, sometimes rivals will go as far as hanging life-like Indian dolls from trees in attempts to intimidate the other team and its fans.

"Native mascots and symbols are all that the kids at my school know about my people. They make fun of me for following traditional ways," said Wayne Crue, a twelve-year-old Native American boy in Astoria, Pennsylvania.

"These fake images make me feel sick inside."

The governing body for the largest college athletics in the United States, the NCAA, is trying to make all universities change their team names. Recently the Bismarck Savages changed to the Bismarck Blaze. However, fans and even some tribes want to fight to keep their mascots the same, whether because they feel honored by the mascot name or just for tradition.

"This is about the Native American people who gave their name to the University of North Dakota and our rights as citizens of North Dakota are being challenged," said Frank Burggraf, a former hockey player for UND. He argues that the native mascot name should remain.

Original mascot supporters say those who are offended by names, pictures and mascots are being too sensitive. "Who cares? I've been called a lot worse. Man up," said Internet commenter and Native American Chris Red-Cloud. "You're going to have a really tough life if you can't just deal with it."

In some instances such as the Florida State Seminoles or the Illinois State Fightin' Illini, the actual Native tribes condone the use of their names and likenesses. Some schools like Stanford University changed its mascot from the Indians to the Cardinal without being asked.

(University Athletics Monthly- Magazine: August, 2013)

COMPREHENSION QUESTIONS

Answer the following questions and write complete sentences.

1. Why are Native Americans angry about some sports teams' names?

____

2. What is the argument to keep the mascots the same?

____

3. What is Frank Burggraf's opinion of the controversy?

____

4. What were the Bismarck Blaze originally called?

____

5. Why would hanging Indian-like dolls from trees be offensive to some people?

____

In a group, write and discuss what you think about Native American Mascots.

Write about what you think about Native American mascots. What are some other offensive mascot names? Why do you think the USA has so many Native mascots? What should they change their names to?

____

____

____

____

____

HERE'S SOME MORE...

Read about culture from across the globe about today's topic.

What's In A Name?

While many people on both sides of the Native mascot debate grew angry, a group of students at the University of Northern Colorado decided to take the matter into their own hands. Or jerseys.

In 2002, these people named their intramural basketball team the Fightin' Whiteys and made their mascots a stereotypical white man from the 1950s who wears a suits and a tie. Originally, the team did this because a local high school refused to change their mascot from the Fightin' Reds. Reds is a derogatory term for Native Americans.

The United States media picked up on the team's name and soon the little intramural team became an Internet sensation. Their website went from a few hundred hits a week to nearly 30,000 a day!

Many people loved the team's name and the tongue-in-cheek humor. "I think it's a great way to let people see how stupid some sports teams' names are," said Sue Reagan, of Pittsburgh, Pennsylvania. "And it's all a harmless fun."

Some didn't find the humor so harmless and were outraged. "I find this offensive. In no way are all white people like this," said Kim Quick. "The original Indian mascots were intended to be honors or tributes. This is just an insult."

The Fightin' Whiteys team members claim this is just a way to fight stereotypes. While most of the original team members graduated and moved on, the website still operates and they sell many different styles and designs of shirts, sweatshirts, buttons and hats. Another interesting thing about the team members, they use all the money they make from the Fightin' Whiteys gear to a Native American scholarship fund. So maybe some good is coming out of this.

(Greeley Tribune- Newspaper: November 23, 2005)

DYNAMITE DISCUSSION

Gather a group and discuss these following questions. When your group finishes, present your ideas to other students.

1. Is the Fightin' Whiteys an offensive team name? Why or why not?

2. Would you wear a Fightin' Whiteys t-shirt? Why or why not?

3. Do you think using Native Americans as mascots is offensive? Why or why not?

4. What are other popular team names that might be offensive?

5. What offends you?

6. What are your favorite mascots?

7. What can be done to fix this mascot problem?

8. Where are sports important? Are they too important?

9. Are names like the "Fightin' Irish," "Flying Dutchmen" or "Vikings" racist?

10. How would you feel if there was a team named the Crazy Koreans?

GET IT TOGETHER

Divide into two groups: one group the Pro team and the other the Con team. Write about the pros and cons of Native American mascots. Then debate.

1. What do you think about Native American mascots? Are they racist or offensive? Why or why not?

____

____

2. Who gets mad about these mascots? Why? Are there any offensive Korean mascots? Where are they?

____

____

3. What are some pros of mascots that use racial stereotypes? What are some cons?

Pros:

Cons:

ANSWER KEY

Unit 1	Vocab Preview	1. accents 2. monitor 3. stupors 4. establishment 5. mingle
	Idiom Time!	1. b 2. d 3. a 4. c 5. e
Unit 2	Vocab Preview	1. acquaintance 2. grieving 3.revenues 4. cremated 5. console
	Idiom Time!	1. d 2. a 3. e 4. c 5. b
Unit 3	Vocab Preview	1. ban 2. parlor 3. convicts 4. popularity 5. opponents
	Idiom Time!	1. c 2. e 3. a 4. d 5. b
Unit 4	Vocab Preview	1. twerps 2. disruptive 3. coddled 4. plethora 5. offensive
	Idiom Time!	1. c 2. a 3. d 4. b 5. e
Unit 5	Vocab Preview	1. mandatory 2. outrage 3. advocate 4. emitting 5. vices
	Idiom Time!	1. b 2. a 3. d 4. e 5. c
Unit 6	Vocab Preview	1. motorists 2. ignited 3. intersection 4. violations 5. discredit
	Idiom Time!	1. c 2. d 3. a 4. e 5. b
Unit 7	Vocab Preview	1. colossal 2. engaging 3. connoisseurs 4. vendors 5. entomophagy
	Idiom Time!	1. a 2. e 3. d 4. c 5. b
Unit 8	Vocab Preview	1. infuriates 2. boycott 3. disciplinarian 4. scrolling down 5. cache
	Idiom Time!	1. e 2. d 3. b 4. c 5. a
Unit 9	Vocab Preview	1. slogan 2. mistranslated 3. widespread 4. botched 5. derogatory
	Idiom Time!	1. a 2. d 3. e 4. c 5. b
Unit 10	Vocab Preview	1. vain 2. procedure 3. cut-rate 4. peers 5. liposuction
	Idiom Time!	1. c 2. e 3. d 4. b 5. a
Unit 11	Vocab Preview	1. cheapskates 2. drive-through 3. metalheads 4. odds and ends 5. bestow
	Idiom Time!	1. d 2. a 3. e 4. b 5. c
Unit 12	Vocab Preview	1. everlasting 2. grueling 3. redundancy 4. vetoed 5. accessible
	Idiom Time!	1. c 2. b 3. d 4. a 5. e
Unit 13	Vocab Preview	1. ferocity 2. controversial 3. masculinity 4. mascot 5. portrayals
	Idiom Time!	1. b 2. c 3. e 4. a 5. D

REFERENCES

Myeong-Hee Seong and Casey Freeman. (2012). *Office Talk: Working in an English-Speaking Office*. Seoul. Baeksan Publishing.0

The Right Age for Alcohol: Colorado Daily- Newspaper: November 11, 2012. USA.
Sorry, You're Too Old: Gangnam Gazette- Newspaper: April 19, 2013. Korea.

Disrupting Rest in Peace: Green Leaf Times-Newspaper: March 17, 2013. USA.
Funeral Customs from around the World: www.PointsInCase.com- Website: December 2010. USA.

Tattoo Taboos: Yatap Yelp- Newspaper: March 24, 2012. Korea.
Tattoo Tips: www.TattooTipsFromHays.com- Website: January 2008. Scotland.

That's Not So Bully: The Chronicle- Newspaper: August 24, 2011. London, UK.
That's Not So Gay and That's Not So Retarded: Colorado Daily- Newspaper: July 7, 2013. USA.

Varying Vices: Busan Sun-Newspaper: July 9, 2013. Korea.
A Potentially Dangerous Diet: Health- Magazine: October 2009. USA.

Open Doors for Drunk Drivers: Bucheon Daily- Newspaper: December 24, 2013. Korea.
Say 'Cheese!': Atlanta Weekly- Newspaper: September 1, 2012. USA.

Waiter, There Aren't Flies in My Soup: The Oregonian- Newspaper: February 14, 2014. USA.
Pass the Bundeggi, Please: www.BundangForeigners.com- Website: December 2008. Korea.

Closing Facebook: Yatap Yelp- Newspaper: May 25, 2013. Korea.
Addicted to Facebook: San Francisco Times- Newspaper: February 11, 2013. USA.

Okay History Is Okay!: www.DailyDictionary.com- Website: November, 2010. Global.
Speak 'Yankee': www.DailyDictionary.com- Website: June 2011. Global.

The Right Age to Look Good: www.AtlasofApgu.gov- Website: January, 2013. Korea.
A Deeper Voice for Deeper Pockets: New York Post- Newspaper: May 29, 2003. USA.

Love Is in the Air, Grab Your Wallet: Korean Nuptial News- Weekly Newspaper: August 15, 2013. USA.
The City of Sin... And Love?: www.FunStuff.com- Website: August 2008. Global.

Making English Easier: Tehachapi Times- Newspaper: April 10, 2013. USA.
A New, Easy-to-Use Language!: www.DailyDictionary.com- Website: April 2005. Global.

Not in Our Name: University Athletics Monthly- Magazine: August, 2013. USA.
What's in a Name?: Greeley Tribune- Newspaper: November 23, 2005. USA.